PORTFOLIO

PAISO

Maya Bathija has been a journalist for more than a decade, contributing to magazines such as *Mercedes-Benz India* and *Global Gujarati*. Personality profiles have always been her forte and she ably headed the *Sindhian*, her family magazine, for thirteen years, compiling content and writing a popular column called MayaSpeak. She has interviewed subject experts and professionals in top positions the world over. She currently travels extensively as a lifestyle and travel consultant with *FWD Life* and wants to continue telling interesting stories. This is her first business book.

HOW SINDHIS DO BUSINESS

PAISO

MAYA BATHIJA

PORTFOLIO
PENGUIN

An imprint of Penguin Random House

PORTFOLIO

USA | Canada | UK | Ireland | Australia
New Zealand | India | South Africa | China

Portfolio is part of the Penguin Random House group of companies
whose addresses can be found at global.penguinrandomhouse.com

Published by Penguin Random House India Pvt. Ltd
7th Floor, Infinity Tower C, DLF Cyber City,
Gurgaon 122 002, Haryana, India

Penguin
Random House
India

First published in Portfolio by Penguin Random House India 2017

10 9 8 7 6 5 4 3 2 1

The views and opinions expressed in this book are the author's own and the
facts are as reported by her which have been verified to the extent possible,
and the publishers are not in any way liable for the same.

ISBN 9780143427773

Typeset in Adobe Garamond Pro by Manipal Digital Systems, Manipal
Printed at Replika Press Pvt. Ltd, India

www.penguin.co.in

Contents

Foreword

Sindhis are the descendants of the Indus Valley Civilization, which historians today, after fresh evidence has emerged, regard as the oldest in the world. Yet its rich and ancient culture has mostly gone unrecognized. That Sindhis possess solid business acumen is a part of popular folklore. I am glad that a serious attempt is being made through the subsequent pages to decode this folklore.

Historically, being traders and entrepreneurs, Sindhis formed the financial backbone of our homeland, spanning the western part of undivided India. Professor Claude Markovits, in his seminal work *The Global World of Indian Merchants, 1750–1947: Traders of Sind from Bukhara to Panama*,[1] examines the medieval trading history of India where he outlines that modern banking methods like bill discounting and promissory notes have their origin in the systems of 'hundis' and 'parchis', which were introduced

---

[1]   Claude Markovits, *The Global World of Indian Merchants, 1750–1947: Traders of Sind from Bukhara to Panama* (Cambridge: University Press, 2000).

by Sindhi traders for global trade. Thus, Sindhis were the original transnational business community of India, which managed its businesses successfully despite waves of European mercantile trade and colonial onslaught. My father, late Shri P.D. Hinduja, was the president of the Sarrafa (trader) Association of Shikarpur.

Sindh witnessed numerous invasions for centuries, but Sindhis not only survived them but also thrived despite them. The biggest reason for that was our ability to find opportunity in adversity. The partition of 1947 was catastrophic for the community. We became stateless as we had to migrate from our ancient homeland. Our never-say-die attitude helped us embrace the numerous lands that we migrated to. We built ourselves from scratch to regain our prosperity by being true to our business heritage. When it comes to business, Sindhis are opportunity-centric and sector-agnostic. The community has attained success in many diverse businesses globally because of the focused approach of its members towards profit and growth. Little do others realize that Sindhis are not only wise in terms of earning their wealth but also in spending it intelligently.

We have a unique ability to assimilate into the local milieu, the way spices mix with our rich food and make it more flavourful. Wherever Sindhis went, they contributed to the local culture and society through their philanthropic efforts. For instance, in spite of the hardships of Partition, the education and healthcare foundation of Mumbai was built on numerous well-known Sindhi institutions. My father, the founder of Hinduja Group, also started two such institutions—the Hinduja College of Commerce and the Hinduja Hospital, which today are the pride of Mumbai.

Sindhis are global in their outlook but remain Indian at heart. We have truly managed to embody the ancient Vedic adage *Vasudhaiv Kutumbakam*, which translates to 'the world is one family'. Divisions of religion, caste, community, etc., are alien to us. The Sindhi community is also perhaps the first one to offer equal space to its women in businesses.

Through this book, Maya offers interesting insights into the business philosophies of some of the well-known families of our community. She has been writing for our community for long now, and I encourage her to continue writing such books so that stories about our community reach far and wide. God bless you, Maya.

11 September 2017

Ashok Hinduja
Chairman
Hinduja Group of Companies (India)

Introduction

Sindhis are a community originally from Sindh, which is now in Pakistan. Even in the earliest references, Sindh has been known as a beautiful land, rich in natural resources. Since thieves can only steal from lands of abundance, the inhabitants of this area had their peace and harmony disturbed from time to time by plunderers. From the Mohenjo Daro and Harappa excavations, archaeologists discovered the city structure that ran with underground drainage, and dug up bricks and jewellery, proving that 5,000 years ago a full-fledged civilization lived in Sindh, on the broad plains and valleys of the Indus River.

The Sindhis were predominantly Hindu by religion, but some later converted to Islam and Sikhism. There was a time when some Sindhi families promised their eldest sons to Sikhism, who wore turbans in the same way as Sikhs.

A lot of the Sindhi heritage and history was destroyed by invaders. Chach Namah,[1] the oldest known historical account

---

[1]   Taken from the foreword that Sanjay Deshmukh (vice chancellor of the University of Mumbai) wrote in Prem Matlani's book, *The Indus Empire (History of Sindh)*.

of Sindh, was written by an Arab historian accompanying the forces of Mohammed bin Qasim, who attacked Sindh in 711 AD. It has also been established that there existed Sindhi Hindu dynasties, such as the Samma, Samra, Khairpur, Kalhore and Talpur.

Sindhis were primarily businessmen and traders. Their skills did not naturally allow them to take part in warfare, but they were known for their perseverance and business acumen even centuries ago. The main trading castes were the Lohana, Bhatia, Khatri, Chhapru and Sahta. These castes were occasionally divided into occupational groups, such as the Sahukars[2] (merchants) and the Hatawaras[3] (shopkeepers). The most affluent Sindhis were the merchants who owned trading firms (kothis[4]) in the major towns of Sindh. Eventually, the name Amil[5] was given to any Sindhi who was engaged in government service.

Post-Partition, many of them who moved to India, having left everything behind, experienced much poverty and hardship. And there has been many a proverbial rags-to-riches story in the community.

The early perception of the Sindhworki[6] who had moved to India and lived in Bombay in the post-Partition days was

---

[2]   Anita Raina Thapan, *Sindhi Diaspora in Manila, Hong Kong and Jakarta* (Anteneo de Manila University Press, 2002).

[3]   Ibid.

[4]   Ibid.

[5]   Ibid.

[6]   Meaning taken from Anita Raina Thapan's (above-mentioned) book. 'Sindhworki' was a well to do Bhaiband Sindhi who was a trader and specialized in the supply of local art and craft objects referred to as 'Sindhi work'.

that a Sindhi would do almost anything to make even a small amount of money. If the shops around sold sugar for Re 1 a kg in bags of 50 kg, Sindhi businessmen would buy 50-kg bags of sugar and sell the commodity on the streets for 99 paise a kg. Their price being 1 paise cheaper per kg, they sold hundreds of bags of sugar, making a loss of 50 paise per 50-kg bag. This amazed others and made them wonder why a person would work so hard to lose money. What they failed to realize was that every time a Sindhi businessman sold an empty bag for Re 1, he made a net profit of 50 paise on every 50-kg bag of sugar.

Sindhis were known to sacrifice profit margins for a large turnover. With the exception of the Seths of Karachi, the Sindhworkis of Hyderabad and the Shroffs of Shikarpur, most Sindhis were local shopkeepers and moneylenders. They specialized in the hundi, or bill of discount, with Chennai, Madurai, Tamil Nadu, and Karnataka being some of the main banking hubs. They even became financiers for industries and filmmaking in Bombay. The Shikarpuri Shroffs were dependent on commercial banks for their trading. The rest went on to become traders, cloth merchants and businessmen, some of them in faraway countries.

Sindhi families have been known to migrate to countries all over the world or to send their children overseas for education. After one lot migrated, they would then encourage their relatives to join them, not only so that the relatives could better their own prospects but also so that they could help the family business grow. Sindhis moved far and wide, to the Far East, the Middle East, the Caribbean, Europe, the Americas and Africa. Over the years, their businesses have evolved from trade and finance to export/import, retail, entertainment, computers, property/real estate, etc.

In most Sindhi families, the heirs were—and sometimes still are—exposed to the family business from childhood itself, creating in them business aspirations at an early age. Sons were expected to earn even while they were studying—what is now known as 'to shadow'. They happily learnt the ropes of their family business, but sadly, formal education was never encouraged among the community, as it was thought it was not in the 'Sindhi blood' to excel in academics. Most Sindhi families felt that the time spent on acquiring an education could be better spent on earning money. They believed that inherent business sense could be cultivated by practice and experience and not necessarily through formal education.

The general sentiment in the community has been that a Sindhi's purpose in life is to make money. Personal satisfaction only comes when wealth is accumulated. This reflects in the popular association of Sindhis with bling, a perception that has evolved from fact. For years, many Sindhi businessmen have felt the need to display their wealth because businessmen require a constant supply of large-scale credit, and that can only be attained by presenting a picture of success and abundance. Also, for a Sindhi, success depends hugely on what the community thinks of him/her. An ostentatious display of wealth in the community is still considered the hallmark of one who has achieved great success, and hence one still hears of extravagant Sindhi weddings and festivals.

Prestige follows success, and Sindhi businessmen beget all this from the social, business and religious organizations of the community. Most Sindhis recognize that because of the nature of their occupation, they can spend a part of their wealth on the community. Donating to charity is thus entrenched in the Sindhi psyche. Sindhis also have a tradition of following the advice of spiritual leaders within the community, such as Dada Jashan (Sadhu Vaswani Mission, Pune). But most Sindhis do not make anonymous donations. The donations are usually made in the name of a parent, or under some family name, thus bringing the donor prestige among the community.

Sindhi women also occupy a unique role in the community. They are bound by cultural expectations and social training as homemakers. The general notion that Sindhi women limit themselves to domestic chores has definitely changed in the last few decades. They saw a role in their husband's businesses as an extension of their roles at home. They soon moved and evolved out of that environment to supplement the family income. However, taking good care of the home with hired help while also working at their business, putting in time at a satsang, socializing, playing cards and being part of a kitty party soon began to define how most Sindhi women spent their time.

Through these activities, the women would pick up the dynamics between the different families in the community and also any helpful information that they could pass on to their husbands. Women in Sindhi families also acted as sounding boards for new ideas or for resolution of any issues faced in the business. The culture in most families was to sit down together for a drink and discuss all kinds of matters, mostly business—and this was how female members of the family were inducted into having a drink or two. The girls were not differentiated from the boys in the matter of getting them involved in work, at least in the more recent years. Today, Sindhi women are an integral part of the business world, and sons and daughters are trained at the same time from a very young age.

There are some characteristics that most Sindhi business families share. Ownership of the businesses usually lies with one individual or within one family. It was not common to have partners who were not kin. Very few Sindhi businesses are publicly listed companies or professionally managed. It's actually rare to see a joint family engaged in business together over two generations. Partnerships between brothers are not known to last too long. All this may be the result of Sindhi values and the absence of professional training.

Sindhis living outside the country are almost always self-employed, and Sindhi employees usually share the same mindset as their employer. These employees see their employee status as only temporary and nurture ambitions of becoming their own masters.

But all this has changed with time. While writing this book, I discovered how Sindhis have evolved with the world. Having met and spent some time with the Harilelas in Hong Kong, breaking bread in their mansion with their wives and seeing them in their offices in Kowloon, I saw how they were able to prove to the world how 100 members of the same family could live under one roof, lead different lives and pursue different businesses. As a community, Sindhis have proved that they are adaptable, can live anywhere in the world and can change to survive in business.

The Lakhi Group—the diamantaires' diamantaire—came across as brothers-in-arms, living apart but running the same business all over the world, sharing, caring and maintaining the same values, morals and charitable interests as a family.

Harish Fabiani broke all the rules by becoming one of India's first-ever individual angel investors. Unlike a family-run Sindhi business, his company takes on a very professional approach to every business it is invested in. From dabbling in technology, Fabiani ventured into real estate and even has hospitality on his mind.

Jitu Virwani of the Embassy Group, the Bengaluru-based billionaire, who in the last two decades has emerged as the largest office-space landlord in India, is also in the residential space. Entering industrial parks and warehousing, he has proved that a totally professional set-up is the only way a business of this stature can survive successfully. Meeting with him in his various tech parks and actually watching his sons shadow him on his business meetings, seeing him with his horses in his riding school, gave me a complete picture of the corporate Sindhi.

Ramola Motwani of Merrimac Ventures shared with me her story of how a woman can dream and reach the same heights a man can in the world of hospitality and real estate. She also exemplifies how educating the next generation can change the whole business horizon for a group, and how being corporate can enhance business practices. Her sons have taken on business partners who have only helped them in their endeavours to reach newer heights. The story of Motwanis is a riveting one of survival and grit.

This book will attempt to trace the complex history of Sindhi businessmen and show how five chosen businesses and the associated families benefited from the unique qualities of 'being Sindhi'.

Harilela Family—Gary and David Harilela

The Family Tree

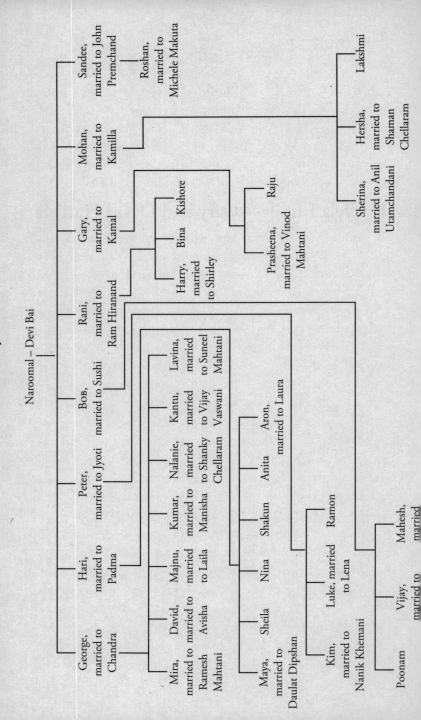

Naroomal – Devi Bai

Introduction

The Harilelas were the first Sindhi family to settle in China and Hong Kong, as early as the beginning of the twentieth century. They braved wars, recessions and depressions (1930) but ultimately came out winners—a trait of the Sindhi heritage shared by many families in the community around the world. But this family never used the immigrant card to succeed. They instead used their courage and patience, laced with an equal amount of determination, proving themselves over and over again.

They went from being hawkers and office boys to starting clothes stores and running tailoring outfits to supply to the army. The Harilelas made their first million in 1950. Though their tailoring business brought them great recognition and a sense of well-deserved success, they knew that garment demand from the army would see a downslide soon, so they ventured into real estate and hotels. Hari, who was the most gregarious of the brothers, was responsible for that decision. He started the Harilela Group in 1959—a great example of the fact that the Sindhi mind is always searching for the next best thing. It is wholly owned by the Harilela family and is a Hong Kong–based private company.

While not everything in the Harilela home was according to tradition, there was a clear recognition of order and duties, if not of hierarchy. The brothers—George (who handled the export trade), Hari (the spokesperson, who handled hotels and real estate), Peter (who was skilled in dealings on the stock exchange), Gary (who worked with Hari), Mike and Bob (who had travel and other interests)—worked together.

They handled diverse aspects of the business; their sister, Rani (now no more), was well-loved in the community for her support of cultural causes. The youngest of them, Sandee, still runs *Bharat Ratna*, the family-owned international magazine for Indians overseas.

The Harilela brothers actually practise what they had been taught by their father—honesty and hard work. Most importantly, he had taught them that money in itself did not mean success and that they had to give back to the community in abundance. They have incorporated the culture and traditions of the country they have settled in (they moved to Hong Kong in 1911), but have at the same time preserved their Sindhi culture in good measure.

People are always in awe of the fact that the members of this 'dynasty' (comprising more than 100) all live under the same roof in a Mogul-styled mansion at Kowloon Tong (1969) and go through the motions of a regular joint family. For most families this has become a feature of the past. Of course, this was made possible because the elders of the family were at the time bound to respect a promise made to their mother, Devibai. The women of the family follow the traditions, speak Sindhi and Gurmukhi, read the Guru Granth Sahib and observe religious days. It is said that if one is lucky to be invited to their mansion for a meal, one can never be sure whom one might meet—which politician, statesman, film, television or sports figure.

After building an empire that boasted sixty-four shops, the Harilelas took on the hotel trade. Their first big venture was Holiday Inn Golden Mile, built in 1975. Today the Harilela Group has extensive experience in hotel development and management. It is a conglomerate that includes hotels, travel agencies and real estate, and has a seat on the Hong Kong Stock Exchange. The group currently owns and operates fifteen properties across Hong Kong, China, the Far East, Europe, Canada and the US.

The group's hospitality portfolio includes alliances with InterContinental Hotels Group, Artyzen Hospitality Group, ONYX Hospitality Group and Commune Hotels. They also have their own Ambassador Hotels in Singapore's Changi airport. They own Holiday Inn Golden Mile (HK), Holiday Inn Resort (Penang), Nova Platinum Hotel (Pattaya) and InterContinental Grand Stanford (HK). They manage The Holiday Inn (Singapore), Thompson (Toronto), Centara Pattaya Hotel (Pattaya) and Grand Coloane Resort (Macau). The new hotels to look forward to from the group are 50 Bowery, New York (May 2017) and The Hari, Hong Kong (2020).

Though the Harilelas carved a niche for themselves in Hong Kong by pioneering the world-famous twenty-four-hour hand-stitched suits, they are remembered more as ace hoteliers and for their contribution to the community. Because they helped rebuild Kowloon and Hong Kong after the war (Dr Hari was the president of the Kowloon Residents Association and the Kai Fong Welfare Association), they were instrumental in helping Hong Kong being called the 'Modern Miracle'. The family has been featured in many magazines, such as *Fortune* (1993), and in many documentary films. Their strength lies in their living and working together.

The Holiday Inn Golden Mile, wholly owned by the Harilelas, has earned the family its major fortune. It was at this iconic property that I was fortunate to have lunch with the reigning patriarch (gen II) of the group, Gary Harilela (eighty-five), who shared bits and pieces of the amazing progress made by the family that he was so proud to be a part of. A gentleman to the core, gracious and kind, he was articulate and reflected the vision of the Harilela family.

The headquarters of the Harilelas are on Ashley Road in Tsim Sha Tsui, Kowloon, Hong Kong, and they house Harilela Hotels Ltd, Ashoka Investments Ltd, Hotel Administrators Ltd, Hotel Restaurant Holdings Ltd, Harilela Foundation Ltd, Hari Harilela Ltd, Well Trillion Ltd and BR International Publishers Ltd.

Impressive to say the least, David Harilela (gen III) was also kind enough to give me time and share his views on his family and what he believes in today.

* * *

In the early 1920s, during the days of the British Raj, Naroomal Mirchandani set off from Hyderabad, Sindh (now Pakistan), on an overseas venture in search of good fortune. Being an astute accountant, he made the long journey alone to Singapore and Shanghai in search of fortunes from trade and commerce.

When he received news from home that his mother was seriously ill, Naroomal applied for leave from the Indian firm in Singapore where he worked, but was denied permission to return to India to see his mother. Since his mother's health was more important to him than his job, he quit on the spot, forfeiting the salary and bonus due to him. He somehow managed to meet the expenses for his passage home.

After landing in Karachi, he sent a telegram to his relatives to say he was arriving in the afternoon the next day. When he reached home he found that his mother had died and the family, without waiting for him, had already cremated her. Deeply hurt, he renounced the family name of Mirchandani and took on a new surname, formed by joining the names of his parents, Haribai and Lilaram. Thus was born the name Harilela, and this is why there is only one family by this name in the Sindhi community.

On leaving India, Naroomal went to Canton with his wife and quickly established himself as an astute trader.

His company, Duru Star, sold jade, amber, curios, silks, antiques, artefacts, handicrafts and rosewood furniture. In the 1930s, the Great Depression knocked down their fledgling business, and Naroomal, his wife and eight children were forced to make the move to Hong Kong to try their luck in the British Crown Colony. And this is where they eventually established themselves as one of the most successful Indian business families. Naroomal and Devibai Harilela had six sons and two daughters—George, Hari, Peter, Bob, Rani, Gary, Mohan and Sandee. They opened a tiny tailoring shop in Tsimshatsui, but business was not good during the war, even though they attended to everything themselves.

In 1945, immediately after the surrender of Japan, more and more British and other Commonwealth troops landed in Hong Kong, and the demand for made-to-order suits and other garments increased. Since the 1930s, the Harilelas' custom-tailoring business had grown continuously, and they now had twenty-two stores that turned out 600 suits daily. The brothers therefore decided it was time to hire more tailors to cope with the orders and to maintain the highest standard of quality. Soon their volume of business grew, as they knew it would, and they became one of the biggest custom-tailoring businesses in the colony.

In 1957, they found that the market was flooded with similar custom-tailoring businesses. Keeping an eye on the future, the group slowly diversified into real estate and hotels. Their flagship hotel—The Holiday Inn Golden Mile in Hong Kong—stands tall today in Tsim Sha Tsui. The other hotels owned by the family are Holiday Inn Singapore Orchard City Centre in Singapore, Holiday Inn Bangkok Silom and Holiday Inn Resort Penang.

Gary Harilela—The Current Reigning Patriarch

Gary is the fifth son of Naroomal and Devibai Harilela. He was born and educated in Hong Kong. After he graduated from high school in 1954, Gary applied to medical schools in London and Canada as he wanted to become a doctor. But since it took two to three days in a small Dakota plane to reach the destinations and long-distance travel was tedious, he decided to give up his aspirations. Besides, his mother, Devibai, also dissuaded him from studying abroad, as she felt there were no relatives or friends there to look after him. Being his mother's favourite, he was not allowed to venture overseas. So instead, he decided to join the family business.

The morals and ideals that guide him and the man he is today are due to the training he received as a young adult, he says. At that age, he took pride in completing every chore assigned to him, following it till the end. He was the one who never passed the buck. Quite aware of the impression that people had of him, that he was slower than the rest, Gary would always do everything to utmost perfection.

Gary is grateful that he started in retail, spending endless hours on his feet, sometimes all seven days of the week, patiently learning how to interact with people and dealing ably with different minds. Over time, he moved into exports and the mail order business that the Harilelas became pioneers in, finally stumbling into hotel construction. There he discovered that his forte was administration, since by now he had mastered the art of understanding, managing and interacting with people.

His affable wife, Kamal (an erudite woman from Mumbai), recounts the early days of their marriage, when she actually saw him only post ten every night and only on half-days, even on Sundays. A gentle, caring husband, he never brought work home, but gave into family Sundays only after his daughter was born. An as understanding spouse, Kamal supported Gary in achieving everything he aimed for. On his part, Gary offered her happy days with their close friends and sailing holidays. They made a world of their own in Hong Kong, retaining a connection to their roots, conversing between themselves in Sindhi and instilling the Hindu way of life in their children.

The next generation—a daughter (Suni) and son (Raju)—has carved out its own path, choosing to set up business outside the Harilela Group. Raju made his fortune as a restaurateur at an early age. At thirty-two, he became the CEO of Inntempo Hotel Development Strategists, involved in the development, planning, operational projections, implementation, co-ordination and execution of hotels. This gave him a chance to apply to Cornell University. But he sold his empire and moved to Switzerland, from where he still consults under the auspices of Atsara Properties Ltd and Harilela Properties Ltd. An apartment is still saved for him at the Harilela Mansion, and Hong Kong is still called home.

The Harilela family provides a classic example of how one generation can devote all its time to creating an empire while the next can decide that too much is too much, and that a creative life is what it needs to be happy. Despite the difference in their approaches to business and vocation, members of the Harilela family embody the fact that the Sindhi brain is always at work and looking to succeed.

Gary's experience as a salesman in the tailoring shops was the best training he received, as it involved meeting customers from different countries. He had to communicate with and understand them. In the process, he learnt how to be patient as some customers were difficult. The motto was 'the customer is always right' and had to be handled cleverly.

Gary next tackled the mail order business that made men's suits. Customers ordered through mail, and Gary supervised operations to ensure the orders were executed perfectly. Then he moved to the import and export department, where he learnt how to prepare documents for the shipping of goods. By this time the family had bought a piece of land, and he was made the project manager, where he acquired knowledge of building, construction, air-conditioning systems and engineering, among other activities.

Subsequently, the burden of completing the Holiday Inn fell on Gary. He looks back on the building of this iconic project with immense pride. He had floor after floor built in such a way that business did not suffer. Gary hired one contractor to complete one floor, while another started on the next. After a point, the hotel began operating even while it was being constructed. This was essential as they needed a cash flow. The management was hesitant about opening the hotel to guests at such a time and brought up many excuses, such as the noise and the danger of injury to guests since the workers were still around, but Gary knew that it was the only way forward and toiled on.

Gary took on the responsibility of any damage by offering third party insurance, saying their operations would solve the issue of shortage of rooms in the city. A professional who was educated by the book would not have understood the need to start so early, but Gary did. It was his hardwired Sindhi instinct that helped him convince everyone that the noise factor could be taken care of, since the workers would work while the guests would be away shopping on the Kowloon strip since the hotel was so strategically situated. At night the workers would not be present, so the noise factor would be eliminated. And if anybody complained, he or she would be offered a concessional rate. They lived by the principle that the customer was always right and had to be satisfied. This was the Sindhi way of doing business— against all odds. Gary turned out to be a natural engineer and negotiator, all rolled into one, even without formal education in either.

Articulate and humble, Gary has maintained the family values and strongly believes that business should always reap profits. He proudly shares with everyone the success stories of his ex-employees who have created their own businesses now. The Harilelas always made an effort to improve the fortunes of other people while they sharpened their own business acumen. Even today Gary insists that ex-employees charge him more than the cost price, simply because everybody has a right to earn. Gary says this is the way his family has always been taught to treat people.

Being the patriarch at the helm now, he sees the same values in the third generation and hopes that the future generations will follow the same principles in trading and in all their interactions. He and his brothers decided that since they had had very little education (because of the different times and circumstances they grew up in), they would extend more than the bare minimum opportunities in education to the next generation. Gary fondly remembers his mother, Devibai, who always said to them that they should invest in humility despite having enough money. She also wanted to ensure that they left behind the legacy of a good name. Gary was strongly influenced by his mother; whose resilience in most matters helped him form his opinions.

Gary maintains that Sindhis respect the Harilela family simply because its doors have always been open to them. His brothers, George and Hari, handled all the charitable contributions of the Harilela clan. Out of whatever was earned, a certain percentage was contributed to different causes. George made sure that a large chunk was sent to India, in the form of aid for education (schools) in Gujarat, for mass weddings and for sewing machines for the underprivileged. Hari would oversee the money that was donated to charities in Hong Kong from the Harilela Foundation.

Being from such an illustrious family, it was almost natural for Gary to become a part of the Hong Kong government. The family mostly gave to the city of Hong Kong, because they believed they should be able to help the city where they had earned their money. They have changed the perception of native Hong Kong citizens about Indians—that most Indians make money out of Hong Kong but send it back to their own country. So by giving to charity (to orphanages, the elderly and school scholarships), they continue to contribute to Hong Kong. Thanks to this attitude the Indian community is well respected in government circles.

Despite being in his eighties, Gary still strives hard to grow the empire. The family fortune is so large that future generations can possibly survive on it for the next twenty years. But Gary is quick to add that money has never been their need, but maintaining their name consistently has. Responsible to a fault and punctual to the T is Gary's character.

A day in the life of Gary Harilela goes like this. He rises early (at 6 a.m.), exercises, eats his breakfast, and reads the newspapers to keep abreast of the world's happenings. After prayers in the family mandir, Gary goes to office, every single day. Once at work, he checks the accounts. The Sindhi way to a successful business is to constantly see that the accounts are in order. Earlier, Gary's older brother, the late Hari Harilela, used to adeptly handle this for all of the family businesses. He was a mathematical genius when it came to this, and Gary partly acquired this trait as he worked as his protégé. Gary now manages the accounts of all the group's hotels around the world, including those in London, Singapore, Bangkok, Penang and Canada.

Gary is also the honorary consul of the Republic of Niger (Hong Kong SAR). For his devoted services to the country, he was honoured with its highest award, The Chevalier de Ordre du Merite du Niger from the president of the Republic of Niger. The ceremony took place at Holiday Inn in Hong Kong. The ambassador came from Beijing to confer the title on him and the ceremony was well-attended by many members of the diplomatic corps.

His civic and social service track record is also impressive. In 1996, Gary was appointed Justice of the Peace by the Hong Kong government for his service to society. He has also been appointed on several government boards and advisory committees.

Gary is highly respected by Hong Kong Special Administrative Region (HKSAR) and People's Republic of China governments. He was one of two Indians (the other being his older brother, Hari) to be appointed to the selection committee responsible for recommending and electing the candidate for the position of the first chief executive of HKSAR and for the selection of the sixty members of the Provisional Legislative Council in 1997 when Hong Kong returned to the People's Republic of China. Later, this body, for electing the second chief executive and subsequent chief executives of HKSAR, was replaced by the election committee. Gary has been a member of this committee at each of the chief executive elections held since People's Republic of China resumed its sovereignty over Hong Kong.

Life in the Harilela Mansion

It is well known that most of the members of the Harilela family live in the famed 100,000 sq. ft mansion in Hong Kong. A monument that took three years to plan and one whole year to build, it is an embodiment of a promise made to Devibai that all the brothers would live under the same roof. The mansion still stands tall and is run like a mini hotel, with a resident manager et al.

Today this super-luxury mansion known for its sheer opulence is inhabited by four generations of the family in the midst of the overcrowded, bustling city of Hong Kong. To accommodate the burgeoning family, including everyone's partners and their children, an annex (eight apartments) had to be built. The main home consists of apartments for the first generation of six brothers and their families, extending to forty bedrooms. The Harilela clan consists of 112 members in all.

The dome at the grand entrance is copied from those of old palaces in India. The lobby with its beautiful fountain is sometimes used. There is a multi-faceted chandelier here, along with a spiralling staircase rising almost to the height of the mansion. A Mexican artist has done murals on the ceiling. The ground floor leads to a Japanese garden and a turtle pond that are used for parties and barbeques.

The Mogul room is fashioned straight out of the sixteenth century, with its carved arches, lounges and divans, as one would find in old palaces. The coffee room and bar have high ceilings, brass grills and a huge carved mirror. The highlight of the Mogul room is an artistically carved chair of pure silver that looks like a throne, complete with a canopy. The honourable Maharaja of Mysore presented this antique piece to the first viceroy of India. The Harilelas acquired it from the London Museum later. All the functional rooms in the mansion are designed differently and are spacious enough for a 300-strong wedding.

For family gatherings and smaller functions, there is a dining room, whose table is fitted with a top of 14x4 ft. acquired from Pilkington, London, which was sent to India to be engraved in gold. The mansion has a centralized kitchen, where the menus are decided a month in advance, and the food is sent to the floor pantry of the adjoining family apartment. Each apartment is equipped with a mini kitchenette. However, menus can be changed and added. All raw meats and fresh vegetables are bought the same day they are cooked. A lot of planning has also gone into the centralized air-conditioning, the heating, the hot water system and electricity supply in the Harilela home.

The first and second floors contain the eight apartments for the brothers. On the first floor is the temple or prayer hall known as the 'Durbar'. It is easily the most important room in the whole house. Functional from 6 a.m., the women of the house lead the prayers here, taking turns through the week. A board lists their weekly turns. A complete ritual of bathing the idols, reading the holy scriptures and conducting the *aarti* is followed. As a religious Hindu family, the Harilelas observe all the holy days. Prayer music is piped to everywhere in the mansion, to the corridors and car park, from 6.30 a.m. to 8.00 p.m. All family ceremonies are conducted in the Durbar.

As the family expands with time, marriages bring others into the Harilela Mansion. The annex is available to the newly married as an optional residence and is accessible by a single entrance from the main house. It houses eight apartments and twenty-four more bedrooms, and has its own living, dining, independent kitchen and laundry facilities. Their garages house their own cars, but parties are still hosted in the main house.

The second generation didn't envisage the entry of future generations. But as we see it today, the mansion houses not only the third generation but parts of the fourth and their daughters and spouses too. But since a few members of the fourth generation have received their education from across the world—from the US, London, Paris and Switzerland—one has to wait and see if they would want to continue this tradition of living as a joint family. The unity will surely depend on the choices they make.

David Harilela—The Third Generation

George has always been regarded as the family's figurehead. David, his son and heir, says, 'The way I visualize the strength of my family is that my father, the eldest, was the cement, and my uncle, Hari, the bricks. One cannot build a strong building without bricks and cement. Dad was the spiritual leader and Uncle Hari the financial leader. It was a great combination.'

A second-generation citizen of Hong Kong, David is tall and handsome and in personality completely candid. Quite the self-made man, David reveals that he was the first Harilela to go away to university (that did not come without opposition, of course). The elders felt if they could become so successful without a university education, why couldn't he? The Sindhi mindset has always been to save money and to do the best one can under the circumstances. But it didn't take long for this persuasive young man, born and brought up in Hong Kong, to convince them that the University of Southern California (USC) was where he wanted to go. So it was a course in business administration for this CEO of Harilela George Ltd, who is also the director of Hotel Holdings and Harilela Hotels Limited.

USC in Los Angeles was David's first choice, even though he was going to trade his interest in music for business. So setting his rock star dreams aside for the sunshine and beaches of southern California, David went on to become a business school graduate (1974). But after that he went back to his father's business. In spite of the fact that David admired his father and loved him dearly, his independent streak did not fade away.

That was what had got him into music in the first place. Making money along the way to support himself also became very important to David, despite being a Harilela offspring. If stories are to be believed, there was a time when George gave his son, David, a mere HKD 30 a month when he was in high school. Having no choice, David took it happily and decided to earn more for himself by singing in his own band, just to prove to his father that he was a capable man. David has always believed that it is better to give and contribute rather than just collect. Growing up in a wealthy family did not mean that he shied away from trying out different jobs. In college, he took on various jobs, working as a hotel reservation clerk, waiter, cashier and receptionist.

Birth of an Entrepreneur

Soon after he joined the family business, David realized that all the processes were already in place, and it would need a lot of pushing and pulling on his part to show his worth. His younger brother was already finding his feet in the custom-tailoring business, but since that was just a spin-off from the family business, they decided they would start something different in retail in the line of fashion. David, completely candid, says they were 'doomed to failure' in their first endeavour. He laughs, saying, in retrospect, they were underfinanced, poorly informed and, moreover, it had been a very bad move. They were definitely not ready for the fashion business, and David realized that in future he would have to rely on his own intuition rather than on anybody else's. David was the oldest of the three brothers. After their initial loss in the fashion venture, his brother Maj moved on to his own business, and the youngest of them, Kumar, went on to look after the family's hotel interests in Bangkok.

Gauging the scenario at the time and being a go-getter, David decided to help the family's flagging export business, the losses of which were estimated at HKD 33 million in 1984. He wanted to take over what was left of the company. He paid HKD 11.5 million to buy it completely (using an overdraft facility). Nobody knew that for all his talk he had merely HKD 30,000 in his pocket. His responsibility, he stated bravely, was to pay the interest too. At the time, the prime interest rate in Hong Kong was 17 per cent. This was definitely a tough goal to strive for, as his family had offered him this company for free. David had always been a dedicated family man and felt his family was not bound to give him this company for nothing. His plan was to pay his father back in one year. But it took him two years instead. David kept his word and paid back his father in full, with every cent of interest.

David left for South America to give vent to his creative streak. He packed three suitcases containing 60 kg of catalogues, and samples of watches, garments and toys. Equipped with just a few random names and contacts, some Spanish phrases and a little help from a friendly hotel phone operator, David jumped right into the fray, looking for buyers.

Taking his wares to the merchandisers directly finally did it for him. Based on the good advice of his hotel telephone operator, he skipped the part of waiting for buyers to come to him. The work was hard, but the effort paid off. He was rewarded with very good margins and great profits. He came back with orders worth HKD 11.7 million in just two months' time. More importantly, he built a client base with whom he could start and build his business, people who would pay and buy regularly. He was mean and lean in mind and body, and he travelled economy to boot. With him there were no excesses. He was thrifty. His only shame was that his father tried to pay his bills when his biggest client defaulted, but David sorted that out all by himself using his creative financing skills.

David is also quick to share his experiences of failure. He recalls the time when he and his friend, Richard, started a huge leather business, acquiring leather from Chennai and Bengaluru in India. One day Richard suddenly disappeared and David found himself facing potential losses of $1.3 million in monies owed.

When David finally found out that Richard was sick with cancer and had also bought his wife a million dollar house, he moved to New York to see how he could resolve this matter. David realized that Richard had created a huge inventory as security for himself and his family while he sought treatment. Staying in New York for several months, David recovered some of that inventory, but Richard's wife continued to be unbending. She even refused David's offer of a house valued at $500,000 to help her husband reduce his debt to David.

So David, along with his wife, moved into Richard's home for a month or so, and worked with Richard to recover his money. As soon as Richard was pronounced cancer-free, his wife presented him with divorce papers. Consequently, Richard died of pneumonia and probably heartbreak. Now the house was totally out of bounds. Stressed about his fate, David went off to visit a dear friend in Bermuda, who offered him $500,000, interest-free, to help him meet this loss and to just forget it all and go home.

Not one to accept any money from a friend whom he didn't know how to repay, David refused this help. He decided to go back to Hong Kong to the business and work to recover the losses. What he learned from this whole experience was that one must always concentrate on solving the problem at hand and not wallow in one's defeat.

Starting Over

David started a company called HGL (Harilela George Ltd) that launched the first international multi-category licence for a major sporting event. It was the first ever attempt by an Asian company to do so in regions like Europe, Africa, the Middle East and Mexico. This experience made him a licensing expert as he took on prestigious names, such as Disney, Warner, Sesame Street, Noddy and Batman.

As a result, consulting became David's niche, and he began to advise companies in America on franchising opportunities. He even served as a non-executive director for Vision Tech. An astute businessman today, David manages the entire family's trading business, together with his licensing, franchising, manufacturing and exporting businesses.

All this led to the creation of the David Harilela Group (DHG), a global conglomerate of businesses. HGL was the original flagship company of the group. DHG was known for promoting sports-licensing brands and for its unique 'store in store' display concept, which consisted of small booths in big department stores or malls. HGL specialized in developing and producing exclusive products for clients. With the help of its in-house engineers and designers, it solved technical problems and turned ideas into reality. David says, with a glint in his eye, that their proudest achievement was when they got a very complicated electronic toy product from the concept stage on paper to the shop shelf in just 140 days. David is also one of the directors of Harilela Hotels Company Ltd, along with Jyoti, Bob, Gary and Kamilla. Dr Aron Harilela heads this company as the chairman and CEO.

Philanthropic Pursuits

It's clear that his father was his idol, as David proudly says that he wrote poems and even a special song once for him. He understood his father's good heart and knew that whenever priests came to take donations from George they took advantage of his generosity and kind soul. Though he argued endlessly with his father about such things, he never left his side and did business just the way his father wanted it, by giving in most of the times. George was known to trust everyone easily and gave people credit too, the primary reason for the group losing a lot of money.

David started a trust two years before his father died, and called it the George and Chandra Harilela Charitable Foundation. To this day he respects all the notable charity initiatives of his father's, such as the Kanyan Daan Trust, which financed mass weddings for women in India who could not afford a dowry or the wedding expenses. Though David never understood this archaic and patriarchal system of giving dowry, George felt it was a small price to pay for motherhood. David stood by his father's decision, regardless of his own feelings on the matter, reminding himself that helping people with their wedding expenses also meant easing their financial burden. George also began the Harilela

Khubani and Harjani Public School, a fine institution which still stands in Ajmer.

Quitting his band in the 1970s didn't exactly extinguish David's love for music. His guitar is his constant companion, and he is always willing to perform at charity events, having done it for Lifeline Express, Changing Lives Foundation, Orbis and the United Nations. He also currently fronts a band of superstars who entertain to please.

A Lifelong Association with the Rotary

All the elders of the Harilela family, as well as George, were Rotarians. They were all past presidents in their own districts. David joined the Rotary in 1999, and till date remains an avid performing member. He has been awarded and has received many citations for being an outstanding citizen. David's skills have been many, but his fundraising prowess came to the fore at the Rotary.

The Gift of Life Project was what caught his attention first. For this project one had to raise funds for children in China who were born with a hole in their heart. He realized that he could change someone's life by paying just $3,500 for an operation. This started David's tryst with fundraising and the Rotary.

For the Hepatitis B fundraiser that he chaired, he raised over HKD 1 million by just premiering Jackie Chan's movie *The Tuxedo* (2002). That led to many smaller successful events, and David became the 'district governor 3450' for 2011 for Hong Kong, Macau and Mongolia, following his uncle, Dr Hari Harilela, who had occupied the same post in 1965–66.

David launched many charitable projects on his own, such as the Cleft Lip and Palate Project for young children in the Philippines. His unending efforts with the Rotary helped him network for his business too. Sindhis are quick to realize that sitting behind a desk is not the only way to conduct business. So even at a charity event, business simultaneously happens for the most part.

In 2013, David took up the position of Rotary Public Image Coordinator (RPIC) for zone 10B, and 2015 saw him being appointed as the chair for their global rewards member benefit programme. All the money he received was directed towards deserving people, because David believed 'there is never enough money to cure the world's suffering, so we should contribute as much as possible'.

It is clear that David's philanthropic work has kept him robust even in his business dealings. He says, 'Since my father died, a lot more fell on my shoulders; he left me as a trustee for everything—the family and the distribution of money among the family members. At this stage of life, I think I did less business and chose to become more of a financial investor. I still do my own business but trading is just a small part of it. Bonds, shares and such take a good part of my time, since I also invest for my sisters and relatives. Leaving somebody just money does not make sense, the key is to teach them how to generate more money from it. I spent half my life idolizing and following my father and half the time proving to him that I was, like him, a true self-made man. I spent my whole life trying to prove to my father that, in my vision, I was worthy of being his son. I never wanted his money, but to be loved the most.'

David believes that the key to trading is to be creative. He has a designer who creates products for his company. His favourite invention is the Time Jammer, a combination of a boom box and a wristwatch.

The One

David has continued the Harilela family's tradition of charitable work in his own unique way too. He instituted an international humanitarian award under the Rotary International District 3540 because he wanted to look for ways to bring back hope and positivity to the world. This award acknowledges unsung heroes, and over $250,000 is given away annually under it.

A German doctor who went to Africa to help the sick inspired David. The doctor used aid from the United Nations to open a clinic in Namibia, where he provided free consultation and free medicines. One night when he was returning home, he was mugged by some of his patients. But that did not stop him for continuing his work. He went back to work the next day and back to his life of serving those in need. This was an unsung hero, in David's mind. Combining this story with Mother Teresa's work that he admired, he named the award The One.

Till date, this award has gone to more than seventeen heroes. It has been given to people in Africa, Bangladesh and India, but to date only one person has been awarded The One in Hong Kong. To encourage more such heroes in his country, David established a separate award for Hong Kong in 2015. He did this particularly because he considers himself both Chinese and Sindhi. 'Pain is everywhere and where god was good to the Harilelas, there they were supposed to help the most,' is his explanation.

Today, in its fifth year, this global award salutes the unsung heroes who spend their lives helping those in dire need. The cash prize is $100,000 for the first winner and $50,000 for the other three finalists. From the many applicants in the first round of judging, ten are selected as semi-finalists for the second round and then brought down to four by a panel of five judges that decides the winner. The results are kept secret till the announcement is made at The One gala dinner. The One committee has also set up an emergency fund for the exclusive use of The One finalists, should they be in need of it.

David has turned out to be quite the humanitarian, following in his father's footsteps, no doubt. Today he lives in Hong Kong in the family mansion with his wife of forty years and his three daughters, Divya, Davina and Sheeva. David is old-fashioned and headstrong, and insists that they live with him.

His free time is mostly spent with his family (which is very little since he takes his work home). He works hard, parties hard, and still actively runs two charities, with music filling the rest of his time. His day starts early with meetings with accountants (for the many investments) and charities, and ends with his active social life.

My interactions with Gary and David have given me first-hand experience of why the Harilelas are one of the most successful Sindhi families in business today. They embody Sindhi values to the core, and while accepting the customs of the country they live in, they have also managed to hold on to the fundamental principles that are characteristic of the

Sindhi community. Their ability to adapt and diversify, their
keenness to innovate and learn, and their generosity . . . all
make the Harilela Group a force to reckon with. Their legacy
will live on not only through the businesses they have set up
and succeeded in but also through their goodwill and desire
to give back to the community.

Merrimac Ventures—Ramola Motwani

The Family Tree

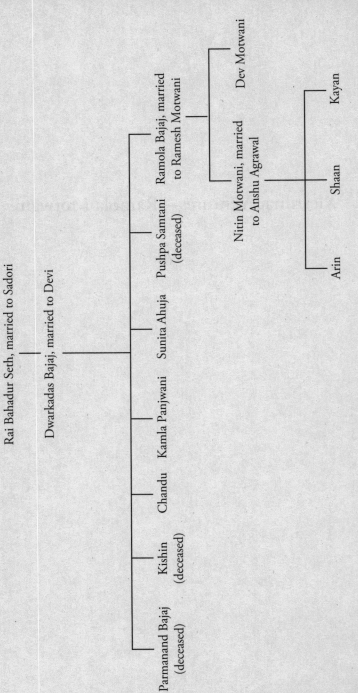

Rai Bahadur Seth, married to Sadori

Dwarkadas Bajaj, married to Devi

Parmanand Bajaj (deceased)

Kishin (deceased)

Chandu

Kamla Panjwani

Sunita Ahuja

Pushpa Samtani (deceased)

Ramola Bajaj, married to Ramesh Motwani

Nitin Motwani, married to Anshu Agrawal

Dev Motwani

Arin

Shaan

Kayan

Introduction

A real estate investment and development company located in Fort Lauderdale (Florida), with projects all over the United States, Merrimac Ventures is an empire today. Its focus is not only prime resort and mixed-use development, it also has extensive investments in multi-family residential condominiums, and in retail and office space. The partners in Merrimac Ventures are currently involved in projects worth over $3 billion, including Miami Worldcenter, which is the second largest project in the United States.

The company is headed by the chairman, Ramola Motwani, who is helped by her two sons, Nitin and Dev. Both young men play their parts in Merrimac Ventures to perfection and also have their own prosperous projects. Nitin Motwani, the older son, is the co-president at Merrimac, while Dev is the CEO and co-president. The company is largely based in Fort Lauderdale, where it employs over 100 people. Merrimac Ventures has properties in Florida, Georgia, Texas and Missouri and other parts of the US.

The Motwanis have played a significant role in the development of Fort Lauderdale over the years. All this was started by Ramesh Motwani, son of Parsram and Savitri Motwani. They are known for buying, expanding and building properties that have increased tourism in the city of Fort Lauderdale. All their contributions, as well as their philanthropy, have made them integral to their

community. They are another example of a successful
Sindhi family who has managed to transform its small
business into an empire with hard work and smart
investments.

Ramola Motwani stands tall and straight as she walks in for the interview, confidence writ large on her face. It's how she handles life too. In the summer of 2017, Ramola turned seventy. It is a befitting time—now that she can look back on the wonderful past—to talk about how she has fashioned her life to live it to the fullest. She still is the chairman of Merrimac Ventures.

We go for a walk in the nearby park. Ramola is a picture of gentleness as she plays with her grandchildren. But everybody who deals with her paints a different one of her altogether. She is still known as an iron lady. It's clear she does not easily let people into her world. Her grandchildren are the only ones with whom she lets her guard down. Ramola's face softens as she remembers with fondness that both her children, Nitin and Dev, grew up getting accolades from their teachers. She accepts that she was a tough mother when it came to their education, but they in turn were excellent students with good attendance.

Ramola has always believed that to go forward in life one needs clarity of thought at all times. It has taken her a lot of sacrifice and selflessness to raise her sons and groom them to take over the empire she has built.

The Beginning

Ramola Motwani has always believed in standing apart from the rest. All Sindhis belong to different sects, and Ramola belonged to the Sukkur community. She married into the Larkana community, to which her college sweetheart Ramesh belonged. Ramesh left India in 1969 to complete his masters in the US. Ramesh (whom everyone called Bob) and Ramola then tied the knot after five years of courtship in 1975 in St Louis, Missouri. Totally self-made, the couple set up an import/export business in St Louis in 1979, selling goods from India and Taiwan in the US. Ramola stood shoulder-to-shoulder with Bob in the running of the business. Perhaps it was a precursor of the life that was to come later. And in a way it readied her for the trials that were to follow.

In the 1980s, when Nitin and Dev were born (eighteen months apart), the couple expanded their business. This enabled them to house a large collection of antiques. They stocked all kinds of furniture, collectibles, fine jewellery, oriental rugs, Italian furnishings and Lladro porcelain. Brought up in a business family, Ramola was always on the lookout for new opportunities. Theirs was a retail business, though a part of it was wholesale, as they dealt with big business houses in the US. Ramola, the multitasker, conducted the buying trips and brought up the kids simultaneously, while Bob handled almost everything else.

It didn't take long for Ramola to realize that they should buy their properties and not rent them, and convinced Bob to do so. So they put a down payment on the building that housed their first business and later did the same for the house they lived in. This was a Sindhi trait, no doubt, as till today one finds Sindhis less inclined to rent and more inclined to buy. The Motwanis own the first building they bought even today, not only because they save on rentals but also because it is a heritage building (most properties being that way in St Charles); it is situated on a quaint little street and open to tourists. Ramola's sentimentality about things highlights the fact that she has built her life on relationships and memories.

It was as early as the 1980s when the Motwanis felt the need to invest on the side in rentals along with the import/export business they ran. They started with a few hundred apartments. They had plans to grow the business, and the business did expand as time passed. It was nothing fancy or luxurious, but it was a business all the same. That was their first brush with real estate.

Imports from India and Taiwan continued to be in demand as big stores were still buying from the Motwanis in wholesale. In early 1984, as their business was prospering, Bob was diagnosed with scleroderma (a rare autoimmune disease at the time). They tried every possible treatment in the US and in India, but Bob's condition only worsened. Ramola continued managing their business and along with her husband taking care of their boys. The times were tough but they never considered moving back to India. All resources and research proved that America was the best option for them.

Ramola had seen her extended family members shed their immigrant status and create successful lives for themselves. This perhaps propelled her to think, live and breathe business. The men in her family had always encouraged education and independence in good doses, as a result of which she had been able to graduate from Government Law College (Mumbai), well equipped for the future.

Out of curiosity, while on a holiday in the beach town of Fort Lauderdale in 1986 (while they were visiting their family), she encouraged Bob to ask a broker to show them properties there. They were living in Missouri, St. Louis, then and saw that Fort Lauderdale Beach was booming with spring breakers. At the time it seemed like a place where they could make a living and where Bob could get some relief from his fast-advancing scleroderma.

The broker showed them three great motel properties— Merrimac, Gold Coast and Tropic Cay, all on the oceanfront. Ramola had to go back to Missouri with the boys because of school, but since they were in a mood to negotiate, they left the broker with a crazy offer, much below the asked-for price. Destiny decided matters for them. The owners of Merrimac got back. Soon negotiations were carried out and a deal was struck. Attorneys got involved, and before they knew it they had a 1950s vintage motel called Merrimac.

It was a great turn in their destiny. They also invested in another hotel at a premium. Their friends joked that most people took more time to choose and buy a shirt than the Motwanis took to buy a hotel. At the time, Nitin and Dev were just seven and six. They moved into Merrimac, but retained the home and business in St Louis. Every two weeks Ramola would commute to their home in St Louis and check with the manager, simultaneously running two homes for some time.

Living in a new city and in a motel full-time had its advantages. The family took pride in its ownership, as they were the first Indians to buy property on the oceanfront on Fort Lauderdale Beach. For the children it was clearly fun, and they understood that their lives were different from those of others around them. The parents made them part of the establishment and allowed them to do chores on the premises.

Bob dreamed of a beachfront property that would sparkle and attract developers, major hotel groups and tourists from all over the world. But they were in for a rude shock when the market crashed suddenly. After a record spring break of 3,50,000 college students, the city changed a few rules, and also banned drinking outdoors. Spring break visitors dropped to 2,00,000 the year Motwanis arrived. Suddenly the dream vanished into thin air.

It went from being a moneymaking destination to a total nightmare, with foreclosures and auction of properties, and prostitution and drug dealing on the streets. To add to it, rumours that the city was not open to students any more went on to hurt business. The $150 million spring break business was questioned, and so were Motwanis' dreams. It was as if life had collapsed in a heap around them. Seeing the climate of Fort Lauderdale at this juncture, the Motwanis not only upped their mental reserve, but also rolled up their sleeves physically and decided to stay through it all. It was not a time for discussions but for pure action.

Neither of them knew much about Bob's burgeoning disease, and that it would finally get fatal. Ramola says that she never felt that Bob would not survive. She gave him the courage to go from day to day and kept telling herself that all would be well. Bob, being who he was, continued being the ever-committed and dedicated family man, and also focused on the business. In the seven short years after he was diagnosed with the disease, he had fashioned himself into a great community leader. The mayor, the president of the Convention and Visitors Bureau and the Chamber of Commerce recognized him for his work. They even presented him with a plaque and honoured him by placing it in front of the Merrimac hotel.

In 1989, the city of Fort Lauderdale did not have a landscape architect and urban planner. So Chris Wren, head of Downtown (Fort Lauderdale) Development Authority, was called to revitalize the beach and transform it from a spring breaker beach into a world-class one. That's when Chris met Bob Motwani, who had taken on the project. He recalls that working with Bob was a very easy-going experience since Bob knew exactly what he wanted. He wanted to change the look of the beach by replacing the cheap T-shirt stores with establishments like stylish boutiques and coffee houses.

Chris helped with the transformation and was blown away at how much Bob wanted to change the look of the place. The first attempt to replace the T-shirt stores with quaint coffee shops was the St Bart's Coffee Shop, which still stands. Chris got to know Ramola better only after Bob's death. That was when he realized that she not only shared Bob's passion but was even fierier. Her focus was mainly on the beach, while Chris tackled citywide issues. They worked in tandem.

Chris has also worked with their younger son, Dev, on the Las Olas Riverfront deal and admires the way he tackled and completed this complicated project on his own, since many big companies had tried and failed. The project had lain dormant for over twenty years and now it's finally going to be revitalized as the entertainment heart of downtown.

Bob started out with a vision for a five-star hotel on the beach. Now of course the skyline is dotted with many more.

Operation Oceanfront

For Ramola, there was no stopping after the first property was bought. The Gold Coast next to the Merrimac became their next big acquisition. They fixed their focus on only beachfront properties as they felt the ocean would always draw people. The Motwanis had a firm belief that the market would revive. It was clearly not going to change from a spring break place into a family vacation destination. With the strength and the love between them egging them on, and their being in the right place at the right time to buy properties, they were destined to survive.

People by now understood them as a well-oiled working team, since they also helped and worked with others in the industry to generate ideas for hoteliers to get through the tough times they all were in. All this was possible because of Ramola's incredible energy and her tireless weekend travel. As Bob's illness advanced, she had to look after certain matters that knocked at her door. They were facing tremendous difficulties at the time, dealing with the downside of their business, acquiring more assets and starting off a second business, Merrimac Ventures.

They leaned on their Missouri business at the time and simultaneously worked hard to attract more visitors to the

Merrimac. Bob, with his knack of getting global tourists, worked persistently and harder than anyone else. By 1992, he managed to attract enough tourists to his hotel in Fort Lauderdale. In October 1994, the Motwanis bought Tropic Cay in an effort to assemble their second beachfront block. Exactly two weeks after the acquisition, Ramola lost Bob, her partner and her loving husband. That was when her life took a 180-degree turn.

Braving the Winds of Change

Bob's passing led to Ramola's decision to shut down the shop in St Louis. She felt as if she had lost a part of her own body. She was totally heartbroken. She had young children with no support system whatsoever, and a business to take forward. The first year was terribly difficult, but she could only put one foot in front of the other in the hope to get going. The boys were just adolescents then and the responsibility of raising them fell squarely on her shoulders. Ramola had promised Bob that she would take care of the children and his vision with equal fervour. This trying time transformed her from a rough diamond into the polished one she is today. She strongly believes that all women should make it their life's ambition to follow their dreams. Becoming a widow should never limit a woman's quest for life.

Ramola set a glorious example with her own actions. She didn't just disappear into the horizon or crawl into bed with grief. She went from being a single working mother to being both parents to her children, bravely taking all that life doled out to her. She knew they had put all eggs into one basket and needed to re-strategize. The economic atmosphere in Fort Lauderdale was very difficult too. Many businesses were shutting down and people were moving away. However, the challenges brought out the Sindhi in her. She saw opportunities where there seemed none, and she did the exact opposite of what was expected of her as a single mother of two young children.

Ramola, using her steely resolve, set about acquiring more properties with her limited resources. The real estate crash of the early 1990s made it nearly impossible to operate on an already distressed beach. But her persistence paid off and her dream survived. She forged ahead with the vision that she and Bob had shared. All the goodwill she enjoyed in the city and the community was because of the excellent relationships Bob had maintained with the city officials. She and Bob had both become community leaders and the city's entrusted development partners. Here she cites all the activities she was involved in, starting from the tourist development council and the marketing and advertising committees to the civic associations, hospitality and lodging associations, and, of course, the beach council.

The next step was to take care of their loan, which wasn't from a bank but from the previous owner of the hotel. She was given ninety days to pay off the loan. As they were friends, she explained to him that it was unfair to ask a widow to get the money from a bank in ninety days when just the applications and processes (which she had never directly done before) would take longer than that. The previous owner understood that she was not using her grief as a tool to bargain with him, so he agreed to extend the ninety days to six months.

Ramola would go every morning from one bank to another, trying to forge a relationship with them. There were twenty-six banks in all where she lived. On every visit she would learn something new, and eventually she succeeded in raising the money she needed to pay off the previous owner. Ramola knew it would not be easy to repay the loan, but nothing is impossible for her once she sets her mind to it. She grimaces at the irony of life as she narrates this incident, because from having no history with banks, she is now chased by all the banks for her business.

A Woman in a Man's World

Ramola educated herself surely but slowly, becoming wiser in the process. Her goals became evident to her. She wanted to get blocks of land together to build large properties on, and to improve the entire face of the Fort Lauderdale Beach. Even earlier, when they had started accumulating properties, the Motwanis were actively involved in the betterment of the community.

Money was coming in from the existing properties and was simultaneously being used to buy more assets. Ramola agrees that her late husband left her quite financially secure, but it was just the urgency of the paybacks and the pressure of having to do it all alone that was unsettling for her. Also, her desire to do the best for her young children was paramount in her mind.

The year 2000 marked the start of her journey, when she single-handedly went to the city and acquired approvals for a 320-room hotel without the help of an attorney. It had never happened in the city of Fort Lauderdale. Of course, before approaching anybody, she had educated herself on the whys and hows, and considering that Bob had maintained relations with everybody, Ramola could ask for help.

The city manager's office walked her through the documentation. She knew that to make a project shovel-ready, she would definitely need approvals. That process itself would cost a couple of million dollars. This led her to her architect, with whom she shared the details of the areas of her property she could build on.

In 2000, the Motwanis finally received approval from the city to build a 320-room luxury hotel that went from being the Merrimac Gold Coast Block (which the family had assembled over the years) to being the site of Ocean Wave Beach Resort and now the Conrad Fort Lauderdale Beach. This 320-room hotel had been the original offer for Trump International. Ramola remembers nostalgically that Bob had stood in front of the property and remarked, 'God willing, someday someone like Hilton will come.' Incidentally, the first developer that contacted Ramola about the property was the Hilton team.

At that point, Ramola found herself in an enviable position as over 100 developers from all over the world wanted to meet her. Fort Lauderdale was finally on the map, and it was getting all the attention it rightfully deserved. When she announced her project, word immediately went out that it had all the right attributes, being a large property on the beachfront, shovel-ready, and with one owner. It created the right kind of buzz in 2001.

Through all the people she met, Ramola extended her knowledge of the business of development. People probably went to Cornell to get that kind of education while she got hers right at her doorstep. Both Nitin and Dev were not included in the initial meetings, simply because they were still at Duke University sharpening their minds. Fear was not an option, and Ramola remembers that at the first meeting she was the one who posed the maximum questions. She adds that business fundamentals are the same the world over. All one has to do is be transparent and have all the entitlements in place. She honestly informed everyone that it was a first for her, but her knowledge impressed the teams that visited.

All Ramola wanted from the deal was that one company build the property so she could cash out and stay on as a limited partner. People still talk about the smart deal that she worked out. She made it completely risk-free—she got her cash upfront but stayed on as a limited partner. The buyers realized that all the other properties on the block had multiple owners and that they would have to spend time dealing with them and acquiring the different entitlements. And time is money in this business. It was at this time that Donald Trump Jr. got involved through the Turkish group, Bayrock, which had an office in Trump Tower. He met with her only once and then the development team paid frequent visits once the deal was struck. The whole building was designed according to Trump's standards and thus titled Trump International. But eventually, the deal did not go through.

The Second Generation

Ramola made sure that both her children got a very good education. They attended Duke University for their undergraduate studies. Both got jobs thereafter; Nitin joined Goldman Sachs and Dev joined Credit Suisse. Then both the boys attended Colombia for their real estate degrees. Nitin had to decide what he wanted to do next, since he was first in line to choose his career path. Ramola gave them the option to be a part of the development team at Merrimac, which would entail immediate learning on the job. She felt that would afford them great insight into the world of real estate since they would sit for meetings with the best developers in the world.

Ramola at the time was still involved with the Trump project. She realized that Nitin was smart and well-educated and she would need a project of that scale to hold his attention. So she asked Nitin to attend the Trump meetings. This was a turning point for him. Ramola knowingly trained him for bigger things. Little did she know that hotel and real estate development was in her boys' very DNA, as was the south Florida lifestyle. In a few years' time, they both undertook significant and transformative projects in Miami and Fort Lauderdale.

Both Nitin and Dev learnt from the times when the deals actually took place, moving to the next tier of understanding that gave them insight into the proper picture of development, where the sky was the limit. Ramola had learnt everything from her family business and so would they, as hardships teach the most important lessons. Nitin slipped well into work mode and they went on to buy more properties for the company. They wanted to create a niche in which value could be created from smaller properties, which could then be sold. As they acquired Waterfront Inn in 2008, which was just next to Tropic Cay, Dev turned out to be quite the frontrunner in acquiring and assembling the second block, which also included Moby Dick and Ocean Wave. Their properties in Jacksonville, Florida, (a long-term rental) and some more assets in Texas and Cleveland (while they worked on the Trump deal) also kept them going. For Ramola, it was easy to manage all this together as she had got a handle on operations over the years.

For Dev and Nitin, it was the transition from doing small business operations to mega development projects that initiated them into the business.

So Ramola turned some things around and structured the next deal so that it suited their ways of working. Ramola adds that working with her sons in both good times and not-so-good times has taught them to function well together. There was no pointing of fingers, no individual decisions, no egos, just plain joint decisions. The criterion has always been—if something makes business sense then it will be done. Ramola says, 'My goal, my vision, my dream, was always to have the family together at the same time, and then let them grow their own wings and explore the world. And I could see that they were moving in that same direction.' She is happy with their choice of business partners, and says, 'It's never about just doing good business, but doing good business with good people.'

By 2005, Ramola went on to invest in more properties like the Best Western, a 180-room hotel with a banquet hall, restaurant, etc. It still exists today as the Sawgrass Inn. By this time Dev had already joined the business. Both the boys had now accepted the way the business worked, and agreed on acquisition of land, attaining entitlements, and finally developing the properties. Ramola remembers a time when every property on the Fort Lauderdale strip, all the way from Las Olas to the Sunrise Boulevard, changed hands except the Sheraton. Today she is proud that her family not only survived that slump but also went on to buy more and more properties and assembled them, sticking to a unique pattern of doing business.

Ramola educated herself in everything, from architecture to dealing with wealthy real estate developers who had begun approaching her for the properties.

By now she knew fully well how to tackle people, as the buyers poured in from European markets, South America and all over the world. All the while, she kept her focus and keenly watched the markets. Ramola learned two important things—the art of patience and the art of holding out—and by doing that helped raise the market rate positively. In 2000, Fort Lauderdale's renaissance became apparent. Over time, Ramola has operated over twelve hotels all over Broward County, predominantly on Fort Lauderdale Beach.

Though Ramola has never been involved directly in politics, she understands it and has indirectly been part of the framework prevalent in her county. When the boys came into the business full-time, Ramola got enough time to take care of other matters of interest. She got involved in many causes and became very active in the community.

In 2008, she hosted a big fundraiser for Hillary Clinton in her house. Recently, she hosted Congressman Patrick Murphy when he ran for the US Senate in 2016. She feels she has a responsibility when it comes to issues that concern the community. She has been involved at the local level, whether for the city or the county, not only participating in fundraisers but also helping with real issues. Ramola feels she is part of this wonderful fabric. 'It is time to blend into this country that has given us so much, and the one way we can do that is by giving back as much.' And the community is grateful for her contributions too. In 2017, on Ramola's birthday, Broward County named a day after her.

Today, at seventy, Ramola has definitely not retired, and anybody who thinks so has another think coming. She is still the signatory and describes her family business as such. 'We have a beautiful system of working together. We all have our own control.'

With Sindhis, it's all about family. Even though Sindhi families may be separated geographically, they are all connected spiritually and emotionally all the time. She says of her sons, 'With my boys I know that when you work at the level they both work at, they are using the best of both worlds, what they watched us doing and what they learnt in the business world in the West. It's an amalgamation of both that has ensured them this success.' From her own immigrant parents she had learnt to remain focused, to persevere and never to take no for an answer.

Ramola is all about women's empowerment. She believes that women are no longer beneath men. She has served as a commissioner, appointed by the CFO of Florida, on the status of women, and has also represented the Sindhi Adhikar Manch at the United Nations. She hopes to take her endeavours on these fronts to a global level.

Ramola begins her day early, taking on the world at 5 a.m. Whether it's just messages on the phone or emails, all her global commitments are taken care of at this time. That way her day is cleared for business and meetings. Ending the day with social commitments makes her life complete.

Community Leadership and Awards

Fort Lauderdale has a stellar citizen in Ramola Motwani as she has been a major mover in beach development and re-development matters. She was also instrumental in securing major sponsors to assist with the cost of updating the wave-wall lights when the city didn't have the funding for it. In 2011, she re-planned the Centennial Beach Fest celebration with the City Commission, starting the annual holiday lights effort on the beach.

Ramola has also been recognized by various organizations. She was named Woman of Distinction by the charitable organization March of Dimes. In 2011, she was the founding chairperson of the annual Jeb Bush Classic Beach Bash fundraiser for cystic fibrosis. The Scleroderma Foundation awarded and recognized her as the largest team fundraiser and individual fundraiser of the year in 2013, and then again in 2015.

Kathleen Cannon, who is the CEO of United Way, remembers meeting her in 2012, and says that Ramola is very invested in the United Way of Broward, being a chair at the mayor's annual gala. She has volunteered her time and energy, and for the organization it's important that they have the right leader, like Ramola. She sponsors events, helps sell tickets, gets her family involved and much more. All the money goes towards education, financial aid and the funding of 100 other similar organizations, initiatives and programmes. At United Way, everyone feels lucky to be involved with Ramola and her sons since they are very well respected in the community and are very influential and generous. The United Way of Broward has rightfully bestowed an award on her.

Being a state board member of the Florida Restaurant and Lodging Association (FRLA), Ramola has worked in collaboration with the hospitality industry and insists that they should offer alternatives to increase the quality and employability of today's high-school graduates by introducing them to careers in food services and lodging.

Ramola has always been passionate about the cause of education. She was shocked when she found out that Florida, being a tourist state, did not have a hospitality programme in any of its curricula. She took the initiative to implement this by becoming the chair of FRLA and bringing it up with the authorities. She has always been a mover and shaker, and believes in action more than just talk. As a business leader she felt these programmes were required and encouraged them even at the undergraduate level. She also coaches the Committee for Education and Talent Supply. The dean of NSU (Nova Southeastern University) says: 'Ramola's passion, energy and enthusiasm towards education showed right through. Not only is she a woman of action, she is also a thought leader. She inspired me to take the lead at my university (NSU) to bring together other thought leaders to create a programme that we are going to launch this fall. It might not have happened without her inspiration.'

Suits, Stilettos and Lipsticks recognized her with their International Leadership Award for being a sassy leader. The Motwani family was honoured with a Salute to Business in

2007 by the Fort Lauderdale Chamber of Commerce, and then again in 2015. Ramola has been a trustee with the organization for over twenty years. The *South Florida Business Journal* too honoured her with the Ultimate Award in 2015.

Thanks to her Indian roots, Ramola has also been the trustee of the South Florida Hindu Temple for fourteen years. An inherent need to assist her community has always been her calling, and today she is the president of the Alliance of Global Sindhi Association. Ramola was also inducted into the *Travel Host* magazine's Hospitality Hall of Fame, and then later in the Entrepreneur Hall of Fame in 2015 by the Nova Southeastern University.

Raj Shah of *Desh Vishesh*, a magazine for Indians, Pakistanis and Indo-Caribbeans, awarded Ramola the title of Community Leader in 2016. Having known Ramola for the last two decades, Raj says that she helps in all community events. She has a dynamic personality, and he feels she should join politics as she is equipped for that role.

The Sant Nirankari Mission named her Woman of Inspiration in 2017. The Fort Lauderdale Beach Council too gave her a Salute to Business in 2017.

Ina Lee (Owner of *Travel Host*)

Ina met the Motwanis in 1984 when she started working with Bob on the Beach Council for Development after the spring break downturn. Bob was taking care of the huge vacuum that was created by that unfortunate event. After he died, she got the family the bronze plaque on the beach. Since then a very good friendship has grown between Ramola and her.

When Ramola took over the business after Bob's passing, the hotel business was struggling and the beach had turned into an unsavoury place. Living above a small hotel, Ramola was working 24x7 and doing whatever it took to stay afloat. She put on a strong front, taking advice from the city manager of the time, George Hanbury, to assemble the first block of hotels. Ramola never gave up, and single-handedly drove beach prices up.

Ramola also worked with Ina on redevelopment of the beach. She spearheaded the march for changing Atlantic Boulevard to Fort Lauderdale Beach Boulevard, refusing to back down on the demand. Ina remembers that when there was a storm that left the beach looking forlorn, Ramola fought for the holiday lights. When the city celebrated 100 years, she was the one who got the city authorities to put up a huge '100' on the beach.

A woman who never took no for an answer, both in her personal and professional life, she was the one who worked behind the scenes, never looking for accolades. She would work her connections and take matters right up to the politicians and the government. Ina says that everyone holds Ramola in high esteem and sees her as a doting mother, a shrewd businesswoman, a mover and shaker socially, a compassionate community activist and a kind and forgiving grandmother.

Chip LaMarca—Broward County Commissioner, District 4

It was 2010 when Chip LaMarca, commissioner of District 4, Broward County, met Ramola and her sons while they were working on the Fort Lauderdale Beach. It was his job to take care of the county's ports, airport, waterways and beaches.

Having grown up in that area, he was very aware of the Motwani family, what they had been through and their success. He met Ramola through Ina lee during the issue of beautification of the beach.

The people of Miami had fought for years to get authorization and approval to put more sand on the beach, as storms erode beach sand. They could not use sand dredged from the ocean because there were environmental ramifications to that. Instead, they trucked in sand from a mine. It was an expensive proposition, and it fell to Fort Lauderdale to do the beautification, which Ramola pushed hard for, knowing that the beautiful beach drew 15 million visitors to it every year.

According to Chip, the Motwanis seem really invested in the county, not only with their money but also with their time and effort. He recounts how Ramola consulted with Dev on everything since he took over the day-to-day running of Merrimac Ventures. Their vision is less individualistic and more about family, he notes. Chip comments that Fort Lauderdale would have probably got built up anyway, but not the way it is now, when it has not just the necessary physical structures but those created by people who actually care. The Motwanis contribute significantly to Broward County, which is a melting pot of people speaking 120 languages.

Manuel Diaz—Mayor

Manuel (Manny) Diaz's association with the Motwani family goes as far back as 2002, when he was the mayor of Miami.

While in the post he met Nitin, a young, educated and successful Miamian. At least 60 per cent of the city's residents are foreign-born, and the city is home to many cultures. When Nitin came to him, initially for work, Manny realized that the Motwanis were a family that lived the American dream and had struggled in order to do so. They loved Miami so much that they wanted to build something special that would be remembered for generations. He could see the fire in Nitin and realized that the young man had a bright future ahead of him. Manny started working closely with Nitin and relying on him for projects meant for the city.

The mayor's office set up a Green Commission in the city that redid the entire zoning code of Miami to make it pedestrian-friendly. Nitin became an integral part of that entire process. They then undertook the rebuilding and rebranding of the urban core of Miami, with Nitin serving on the Downtown Development Authority, which he does till today. He became an important ambassador for the city. Manny says: 'Nitin was more than just a developer, he has always been considered an important part of the team and the efforts that built the Miami that we have today.' Manny believes the Miami Worldcenter being built by Nitin and his partner is the most significant project in the city right now.

As a Cuban immigrant, Manny identifies with the fight and energy of the Motwanis because he feels multigenerational Americans are complacent in comparison. He says, 'With Nitin, I was impressed that he was doing the right thing because there are developers who are motivated only by the money and are not worried about the impact that their project might have on the city.'

Nitin—The Creative Entrepreneur

Thirty-eight-year-old Nitin Motwani, at six foot two, towers above everything. He certainly owns the room. Handsome, distinguished and very much the family man, he is a successful entrepreneur today and an integral part of Merrimac Ventures.

While growing up Nitin was always aware and sensitive of the fact that his parents were working extremely hard. Both the boys saw how difficult it was 'making payroll', and that too when the spring break ended in Fort Lauderdale. Even though they didn't have too much money or credit, his parents still went ahead and bought more motels, knowing fully well that it was the right thing to do. Business had to go on. Goals had to be followed. Throughout their struggle, his parents defined a larger vision—that they were not the family who wanted to buy 100 motels by the highway and create great cash flow. Their vision was to buy great properties that would develop into bigger things. They wanted to leave behind a legacy for their children, one that they would be proud of.

They acquired one block, and while they were acquiring the second block his father passed away. His mother persevered, and they continued to live and work in those hotels. The transformation of the beach was a fifteen-year process. To a child, it was exciting but also very terrifying. Since the markets had tanked in the financial crash of the late 1980s, it took longer for his parents' vision to come through.

Nitin realized it would get harder for his mother since she was a single immigrant woman with two young kids.

But Ramola, he realized, was not one to take anything lying down. To all the people who didn't want to extend a loan to her just because she was a single woman, she proved herself by getting the job done in record time on her own. Witnessing all that, both the boys initially decided not to enter the same business. They left south Florida and went to college in Duke, one after the other, since they were just eighteen months apart. Nitin tried many subjects in college—pre-med, then economics, and even pre-law at Oxford in the summer—but still could not figure where his future lay. When he returned from Europe, he realized most people were going towards investment banking.

He didn't know much about investment banking then, but he got himself a summer internship at Goldman Sachs in New York, where he had a great time. He interned well, so he got a job as an equity derivatives trader, finishing one semester early. That's where he met his wife Anshu. It was a great job, with great mentors and a great love affair, so Nitin wasn't keen to go back to the hotel business at the time. In the meantime, Dev graduated and went to Credit Suisse.

Eventually, Nitin realized that investment banking wasn't a long-term choice for him. He also knew that while he had moved away to finish his education, his mom had definitely upped the game and was meeting with a variety of developers to take on the motel blocks she had assembled. In the early 1990s, one of them was the Hilton Group, but eventually the project didn't move forward.

There was also a rumour that St Regis wanted to set up in Fort Lauderdale. It was at that time, in his early twenties, that Nitin found himself flying down to meet these developers.

He realized that it wasn't just the hotel business that he wanted to be part of. Coming up with a vision and creating something was what he wanted.

Ramola was dealing with Trump International while Nitin was away in Colombia for his masters. Simultaneously, he started interning with the developers who had taken on the Trump project. All through that, he realized that this was his true calling. So he graduated and moved right back home. The Trump deal lasted a whole year, from 2003 to 2004. They did the deal with the developers that were representing Trump and the project sold at $1162 per sq. ft, at a massive premium to the market rate of $800–900 per sq. ft In this case, the developer performed, but unfortunately he delivered only in 2009. For a variety of reasons, the project did not go forward.

Arthur Falcone—Nitin's Partner

At the same time, Nitin also met his current partner, Arthur (Art) Falcone, the managing principal of Encore Capital Management. Arthur had sold his homegrown business in 2005 for a lot of money and was looking to invest. Nitin was there at the right time, right place. They met socially in 2004, and again in 2005 as Art decided to partner with Nitin. Art felt he pretty much understood where Nitin came from since they both had similar hotel backgrounds and family stories. They connected over the same priorities of family and hard work.

In the meantime, Dev went to India and struck up a lot of relationships in the real estate sector. He even rented an office in south Mumbai. But it seemed like the wrong time because many equity and hedge funds from America showed up exactly six months later and sent property prices shooting up. To add to that, there was a lot of bureaucracy, laced subtly with corruption. It was difficult for Dev to understand how to scale up business over time in that kind of market.

In 2006, Art wanted to explore India too, along with Dubai. He sat Nitin down and brought up India, saying he wanted to invest in the country with a local developer. So they acquired a partner in India. Art and Nitin flew to Bengaluru, then Mumbai and Delhi. The possibilities seemed endless, and Art realized that there was a lot of scope for hospitality and real estate in India, but the meetings their local partner set up did not materialize and they did not receive the enthusiastic response they were expecting.

Art talked about the journey to India and said he just did not understand the bureaucracy and cash systems that existed. He was shocked that there was no title insurance and too many entitlements, but he did believe that the growth potential in India was tremendous. On their fourteen-hour return flight, Art and Nitin agreed they were not ready for India because the laws in the country were not conducive to their business. Art draws a comparison to America, where real estate is as clean as any other business because of the laws and regulations. So, at the time Art suggested to Nitin that they focus solely on Miami. That's when they decided to concentrate on the project that came to be known as Miami Worldcenter.

By 2004, Art had assembled pieces of land in downtown Miami and requested Nitin to join the team and run the project with him to create a city within a city. Art seeded the whole deal with the first $100 million. They bought some more land, while Art hired the design team and started the entitlements process. On a global basis, they have a company called Encore Capital Management, of which Nitin is one of the partners and sits on the board. With this company they do projects around the world, theirs being a nationwide platform. They have development worth $6 billion right now that can be used as mixed-use projects, master plan communities, high-rise condominiums, etc.

Then the recession hit America and they slowed down. They bought the rest of the property they required only by 2010–2011. After that they brought in a third party, an institutional investor (CIM). Over 2009–2010, the Miami Worldcenter was ridden with problems, and it proved to be a very difficult time for the group. There were many legal issues and lawsuits that lasted for four years. With two of their banks going out of business, they had to rebuy (in an auction) the paper of the debt from the institution. They faced multiple lawsuits from neighbours who wanted to stop the project, had to redo the government entitlements twice, deal with unions for labour agreements and with neighbouring communities over jobs. For Nitin the trials were non-stop, and Art agrees that in all of his twenty-six years of working, this was by far the hardest deal.

They haven't been able to let out a sigh of relief yet, though they are now definitely more optimistic about MWC reaching completion. Currently they are in the first phase, whose completion will take about two-and-a-half years. It's been fourteen years since Art put together the property. It's a huge project and will take a lot of attention and patience.

Art adds that he shares a lot of the value systems with the Motwani family in terms of the passion and hunger for work and for making things a success. Nitin, in his opinion, is a great warrior; he has resilience, patience and great fortitude. Art often tells Ramola that she must wake up in the morning every day with a smile on her face because she has brought up two really great and deserving sons.

Making Miami Worldcenter a Reality

When the recession hit, two of their well-known banks got taken over by the government. So Nitin and Art had to either continue with their vision or get rid of the land. Art thought it would be a good opportunity to get rid of the land, but when one's banks get acquired, nobody comes forward with money to buy. People thought they were crazy to take on such a big project because at the time there were thousands of condos lying empty. Of course, now they see it differently.

Nitin and Art believed Miami would be the city of the future and that it would become a global gateway city. Behind their decision was the realization that technology allowed people to live anywhere, so people need not live only in New York, Chicago or Boston any more when they could enjoy a better lifestyle, great weather and lower taxes in Miami.

So they repurchased all the 19 acres that they already had, bought an additional 8 acres and designed it as a city within a city so that they could have their own zoning code and taxing district. They started partnerships to develop certain pieces of the land and are now building Paramount Condominiums— apartments, retail and parking garages. MDM and Marriott came in to build the convention hotel. Nitin and Art also sold a land parcel to Hines, an office developer, since they don't build offices.

Nitin describes Art in three ways: mentor, partner and close friend. He says, 'Art made the decision early on that I was going to be his partner, not his employee.' They often joke that people thought they were crazy between 2006 and 2008, stupid from 2008 to 2011 and now that the market has changed, very lucky. But Art has seen it all, and had always told Nitin that perseverance and belief in oneself usually pays high dividends.

At the same time all this was happening, they set up their private equity fund, Encore Capital Management, in 2009. Art is its managing principal. They raised $1 billion to design and build Miami Worldcenter. The equity company has raised billions in assets and has moved on to building in California, San Francisco, Los Angeles, Portland, Oregon, Dallas, Texas, Scottsdale, Arizona, and across the state of Florida. The $6 billion worth of development they have all across the country excludes Miami Worldcenter and investments by the Motwani family.

Land Acquisitions and Progress

For the Miami Worldcenter, Art and Nitin had to buy land from forty-three different people, often concealing their identity to keep the prices down. The second largest project in the country, it is exactly the same size as Hudson Yards in New York. While acquiring the land, Nitin met people who would not accept that they were in a recession. Each story worked out differently. They agreed to some people's prices, but said they would pay them in five years' time. Sometimes they would tell the seller that they would wire them the money the next day itself if they sold on the spot. At other times they would have to send somebody else to negotiate instead of going personally because prices would shoot up if the developer was known. Everything had to be done artfully.

They also had to trust the leadership. Manny Diaz was the mayor when they started on the project, and they had to believe that he would share their view and understanding and give them the flexibility to build something like this over such a long period of time. Nitin says, 'Manny is a phenomenal personality. He believes in Miami just like I do, but he wasn't easy to convince when I first met him, because he was dealing with trust issues too, and had so many questions for us, grilling us about our design, our finance, our involvement in the community. We had to earn his trust.'

It was very important to have him on their side as they had to present their plans at twelve different public hearings. And even though no decision in Miami is ever unanimous, they got all the votes. They spent a lot of time engaging the community because that's how Nitin's parents had done it.

They knew they would have hurdles—buying and assembling land, dealing with a great recession, and with people's egos. No matter how good a job was done in the community, some people would always disagree, but Nitin and Art trudged on to the best of their ability. They were humble, hardworking and young, and earned people's respect as a result. They started the project in 2006, and it has taken them eleven years to reach where they have. Fortunately they have their private equity business and are also very big investors in the project.

Phase 1 of Miami Worldcenter will cost $2 billion, and the next phase, $2.5 billion. All the areas around will be developed at the same pace. Only halfway into the development, Nitin and Art know there's so much more to do. The project is going to embody luxury. They are also building condos for rent, apart from big hotels, small hotels, office buildings, a mammoth $700 million, 1,800-room Marriott Marquis on 5 acres and a mall by Forbes and Taubman.

What they really want to do is create great places, but maybe not on such a scale every time. Not many cities in the world can handle such big projects. Their ideas evolved as they travelled and saw that a city usually depended on a centre, such as the Rockefeller Center in New York (which changed midtown New York), LA Live in Los Angeles and Roppongi Hills in Tokyo. Miami Worldcenter is surrounded by the art museum, the science museum, the performing arts centre, the port of Miami (which is the largest cruise passenger port in the world) and Miami Day College (the largest college/downtown campus). To the west is the Grand Central Station (the first privately funded station in 100 years). And the University of Miami has its medical campus three miles from the centre. 'It's like we are the hole in the doughnut,' remarks Nitin. The uniqueness of the project gave them the conviction to build it. It is similar to what the Motwanis had done with Fort Lauderdale Beach.

Apart from Miami Worldcenter, Nitin and Art are working on 563 ultra-luxury condos in Miami called The Paramount (10th and 2nd Avenue), which have fetched buyers from more than thirty countries. Nitin also excitedly talks about another project in Orlando under Encore Capital Management, called Encore Club, describing it as a big horizontal hotel. The hotel will not consist of tall buildings but will have one-storey, ten-bedroom homes built on 3,000 acres. These would be ideal for people who want to visit Disneyworld with the entire family and to live in a home away from home. The project will also have two water parks, three golf courses, tennis courts and soccer fields, making it a great destination for tourists, because people are now travelling with friends, relatives and families, and this kind of place definitely beats hotels. Nitin and Art are doing two of these in Orlando, one of which is with the well-known singer Jimmy Buffet, called Margarita Ville. Every market is different for the Motwanis since they like to create great things and own them for a long time, as the kind of assets they are building cannot be replicated.

Historically, their model was a fund business in which they had to sell, but a private real estate investment trust (REIT) called Rescore allows Nitin and Art to build and own projects for a long time. So they are trying to create more long-term projects. As a family, the Motwanis are also investing in technology companies that will modify the way people live.

In mixed-use real estate projects, a lot of the work is interconnected. Nitin learnt to be neutral from his parents, whether things go right or wrong. He just keeps going. He's also more careful about taking work home now so he can spend quality time with his wife and kids. Though, when one is an entrepreneur, work is always on one's mind.

Being level-headed in business always has a positive effect on the people one works with. Nitin is a delegator and does not believe in micro-managing, because then one will definitely not be able to scale a business. He does, however, like to micro-manage relationships, for instance, with investors, a mayor or a politician. He enjoys being with people who are better at their trade than he is at his.

Nitin and Art like to have a little diversity in their business, and so do the banks, to avoid another year like 2008. In the US now, everything is so much more complicated in the regulatory and legal environment than it was earlier, simply on account of the size of operations these days. As a result, more partners are needed in a venture. The Motwanis have an incredible network in the US but are always looking to expand to other countries.

Civic Life

Nitin's life is busy, but he is a responsible citizen. He is an executive board member at the University of Miami's master of science programme in real estate development and chairs the DDA (Miami Downtown Development Authority). Nitin was awarded the Rising Stars of Florida Under 40 from Real Estate Florida in 2013. In the same year, he bagged the '40 under 40' from *South Florida Business Journal* (*SFBJ*). In 2014, he was named one of Tomorrow's Leaders by the Real Estate Forum, and also received the Young Leader of the Year award from the Urban Land Institute; he was among the '20 under 40' of the *Miami Herald* and Real Estate's Rising Stars in *Real Deal*.

The year 2015 got him Stars to Watch from *Commercial Property Executive* magazine, Skyline Makers from *South Florida Executive* magazine and Top 100 Power leaders from *SFBJ*. In 2016, he was in the Miami Power 50 of Real Estate Bisnow Power Leaders by *SFBJ* for the fourth year in a row.

Personal Life

They were many times that people thought Nitin was crazy to stick to a project for eleven years, but that's who he quintessentially is—perseverant. He wants his sons to grow up passionate and aware, the way he is about cities and urban living. He says that he didn't have a clichéd Indian upbringing, but his mother knew every single teacher of his. If he and Dev didn't get As, she would want to know why. Having said that, she gave them a lot of freedom to develop their own personalities. But he also attributes this quality to how much he saw his parents work towards all the right things. Both he and Dev knew that their mother was distraught when they lost their father but she never showed it.

She protected and shielded them from all the economic problems around, creating a life they would love. Being responsible children, they started work early in their lives. Nitin has worked as a waiter, valet, restaurant delivery person, room cleaner, front desk assistant, soda machine loader, quarter counter and guest usher at Merrimac, taking it all in his stride.

Nitin shares an incredible relationship with his mother. He can never forget her advice, 'Don't ever be afraid to ask.' From their parents, Dev and he also learnt to give. They used to see their parents struggle so much and yet give for civic matters and philanthropic purposes.

An early riser, Nitin is the father who's up with his kids at 6.30 a.m. He feels some of the best times of the day are when he's in the playroom with them, building Lego and fooling around. He lives in Coral Gables, a beautiful wooded old-world area, and walks his children to one of the best schools in Miami.

He enjoys that he has no fixed schedule and that no two days are the same. At any given time, he could be walking with a labourer on site, having breakfast with a politician an hour later, and looking up a new project later in the day. He says, 'Part of why I did not like life on Wall Street was that I knew that the rest of my life I would be there from 7 to 7.' Nitin is a people-oriented person who loves that his job gives him experience in design, marketing, law and construction.

Every Saturday is date night for Nitin, and on weekends he hardly puts in any work. At least once a year is spouse travel time and once a year family travel time. Quite the romantic and family man, Nitin makes time for everybody and everything. His wife, Anshu, is a senior vice-president at Bayview Asset Management. She is a hands-on mom and wife and deals with everything in her own special way. Having known Nitin now for close to sixteen years, Anshu maintains that they are their own people, independent, and follow their own goals. Anshu went on to work with Blackstone after Goldman Sachs and then attended Harvard Business School. Today she and Nitin have three boys.

Though she has an MBA and worked in hedge funds for fifteen years, she cannot see herself working with Nitin because of their different styles and personalities, she says. While she is very risk-averse, he has to take risks for the most part. Both Anshu and Nitin believe there's only that much happiness that can be derived from money alone. Their primary concern is that their children grow up to be sensible adults.

Anshu says she was totally intimidated by the Motwani family when she first met them because she was aware that Ramola had gone through hardships and single-handedly raised two boys who idolized her. She was, after all, marrying her older son, the apple of her eye. But she got over that soon because of the sense of optimism the family exudes. Ramola, though tough as nails, has a large heart, making her the most amazing grandmother. Anshu has since then fit right into her role as a Motwani and today enjoys it that she and Nitin are deemed a successful couple in Miami.

Nitin is a practical man who enjoys driving his Range Rover rather than a fancy expensive car. Travel, boats and tennis top his list of interests, and he particularly likes skiing in Aspen in the winters and hiking in the summers. Having lost his father at an impressionable age, Nitin hangs on to experiences and never takes anything for granted. He says, 'I'm never not busy; just busy with the things I want to do. It never occurred to me that I would not be successful in persevering through the hard times because everything, including the hardest recession in a 100 years, happened, and here we are! And during that same time frame we were able to raise billions of dollars in capital.'

When asked if he enjoys being in real estate, he replies, 'Of course there are many ways to make more money, but this is exhilarating!' It's the same feeling he gets when he thinks of his mother walking down Fort Lauderdale Beach, feeling proud for creating something. She's been a part of history and he too would like his own piece of sunshine.

Dev Motwani

Dev wanted to be a lawyer since an early age. When he went to high school, he tried a pre-law programme and realized that it was very tedious. People had led him to believe he would be a good lawyer because he was argumentative. Being logical now and good at debating various topics, he realizes that there is much more to practising law than the glamorous side of crafting arguments and being in the court room.

As an adult, Dev knew he wanted to do something in the business world since he had always seen his parents in that atmosphere. He wanted to be an entrepreneur, but definitely not in the motel business. When he was eight he would hang around the hotel playing video games while customers checked in. He would pause to check them in if there wasn't a clerk there to do it. He also knew that he was good at maths because he could calculate the sales tax of the room rent in his head.

Despite the stress of watching their parents cope with many a problem, both Nitin and Dev enjoyed living at the Merrimac. They had their own pool and a life different from all other kids their age. As their parents realized that their future lay in picking up more distressed hotels along the way, the boys decided they would never come back to Florida or get into real estate, because it was all a reminder of their parents' struggle.

When the two of them went away to Duke University, Dev explored studying business. He travelled a lot and took some time off to work in politics in the West Wing of the White House (four doors away from the Oval office) for the vice president, and then for the Al Gore presidential campaign in 2000. He later moved on to work in finance, doing investment banking and structural derivatives at Credit Suisse for nearly five years. The hard work taught him a lot of work ethics, and about institutional and capital markets. He learnt important skills that really helped him later in his career.

When he returned, Dev found the development side of the business extremely creative. He says, 'As a kid, I mostly saw how my family dealt with real estate, never with development. And when I saw how development worked, that's what pulled me away from Wall Street and back to Fort Lauderdale.' What both Nitin and Dev came back to was the Trump deal. In the 1990s, the whole development world had changed. Initially, the Hilton and Marriott groups were building hotels, but then they changed their business model to merely managing for third parties, i.e. the developers would build the hotels for them.

In 2006, Dev was focused on the family portfolio and the Trump project. So he was participating in all the owner and construction meetings on a regular basis. They still had half a dozen operating hotels, such as Tropic Cay, Waterfront Inn and Quality Inn. He was also overseeing the day-to-day management of a couple of small motels on the beach. They had a number of investments in retail properties in Jacksonville, a building in Cleveland, Ohio, and investments in some apartments in Austin, Texas, which were managed by their other partners.

At the same time, the Four Seasons Hotel and Residences Fort Lauderdale Beach project began. It got approved in 2008, but lay dormant till 2014. It will have a 130-room hotel and ninety luxury residences, which the group is looking forward to readying till 2019. After the Four Seasons project got stalled, Dev started to look at new properties, but at the time banks were not lending to real estate. He wanted his mother to have a diversified portfolio. All the major companies in America have investors, so that's when Dev decided to go down that route. That would be one way to create more leverage and thus up the value of Merrimac Ventures.

Nitin and Dev came home from Columbia to experience the worst recession since the Great Depression. Fortunately, the economic risk the family had taken had taught them a lot financially. By this time both had earned their Columbia degrees and they understood all the aspects of real estate, development and different product types. Also, at that time they were already running motels. They went through the experience of seeing the business move away from just property management after their acquisition (with some partners) of the Hilton in North Carolina (next to Duke).

The Motwanis lost money in the 2009 crisis, like everybody else. With the markets down, they had to react and adjust to the new circumstances since everybody in every business type had the same story to tell. They had to protect what was left, adjust their expenses and accept their reality. Fortunately, Ramola and Bob had created a solid foundation, and they could still maintain all their properties even though many others had lost all their assets. Once everything in the market stabilized, Dev saw the opportunity to do more deals.

But in order to do those, he needed new partners as he didn't want to touch the family assets. That's how he found his current partner, Bill Holland.

Bill Holland—Dev's Partner

Bill Holland's investment business, CI Financials, in Toronto manages over $150 billion, making him one of the most important businessmen in Canada. He has been the family's investor since 2010. Bill, the chairman and CEO of his company, says he met Dev when he and his partner were looking for real estate post the 2009 crisis. They were bidding for the Riverfront Project when Bill's partner ran into Dev (who was in his twenties), and Bill decided that he would be the ideal candidate to run their real estate business in the state. Bill and his partner were new to the Miami area, having not really invested there earlier. But they were impressed by the young man who clearly understood real estate and, most importantly, south Florida businesses. Bill remarks, 'We would have probably bought much less and done much worse', if they hadn't met Dev.

Because his family had already done so much business, Dev knew the strip well. Also, he was in the know of people who made decisions in the city. His network was amazing, as were his people skills. He was just starting his career after coming back from Wall Street, so there was a different kind of hunger in him; he was learning everything incredibly fast.

With the Gale Boutique Hotel and Residences, Bill and his partner are developing 129 branded residential condo units and a ninety-six-storey Gale-branded boutique hotel in the middle of a historical property. They had bought it just before they met Dev, and Bill feels they would not have had the solutions they do now, as part of the property is a historical site. If it was not for Dev getting around to the people who handled heritage properties and explaining how well their plans would impact the county, the project would have never seen the light of day.

Today, together they have developments in the Las Olas riverfront: the Four Seasons, The Riverbend, Pembrook Pines, Plantation and Pampanoo. In Atlanta, they have the Chieftain Atlanta, a rental portfolio of 485 single-family homes and town homes. Bill is the investor/partner and Dev manages the business. Bill also remembers how dynamic he found Ramola when he met her a couple of years ago during her induction into the Business Hall of Fame in Broward County. She got on stage and held the attention of a 1000-strong audience.

Bill agrees that a lot can go wrong with the real estate business, but when he is with Dev he feels secure because Dev is very good with solutions. Though Dev travels all over the world, his eyes and ears are everywhere and he works very hard. His kind of ambition sits well with Bill. Dev's USP, besides his capacity for hard work, is that he's always looking for the next big idea. At thirty-six, the world's his oyster, and his projects can only get bigger. Bill is impressed with the values of the Motwani family and how both brothers are truly partners and not competitors.

Dev—The Entrepreneur

Merrimac Ventures was mostly buying land before Dev met Bill, and was doing incredibly large deals. So Dev had to bring in the right equity partners and good investors. Bill Holland was his best option. They targeted key pieces of land and waterfront properties to buy because that's what his family had always done. Over 2010–2012, nobody wanted these properties because the mentality was that nobody would ever build again, or people believed the bad times would take longer to settle. It was clear to Dev that they would have to bring in partners and buy properties in cash. When the markets bounced back they could develop the properties.

Resilience and patience seem to be the names of the real estate game, where one can either make a lot of money or lose a lot of it. According to Dev, the resilient ones were his parents who went through rough times and invested their life savings. As they didn't have money to hire people, they did everything themselves, building everything from scratch.

In 2009, Dev did question his decision to return to real estate after leaving his job at Credit Suisse. He remembers having dinner with an older and wiser friend in real estate, who said to him, 'If you honestly do the right thing and use your twenties to figure out what you want to do with your life, then success will be yours. But the only difference is that some people get successful faster than others.' That stuck with Dev.

Dev felt he understood the advice, because in 2011 everything stabilized for him after he met Bill. In 2012, he bought some properties, and the next year he acquired some more. He began their actual development in 2014. Now with the Gale, Paramount and Four Seasons properties breaking ground, he is seeing the culmination of five or six years of hard work. Dev now knows it was not all for nothing.

Initially, Bill was working with another partner on the Gale project. At the same time, Dev was also trying to buy the property with another person. The investor went with the bid that Bill and his partner had put up. However, Dev met with them, and since he had done all the work on the property and had the vision for it too, Bill snapped him up immediately.

Real Estate Deals

So the only deal that Dev ever lost brought him everything good. Over time, as he acquired their trust, they became partners. Six months after the first deal, they moved on to partnering with him on the 3.7-acre Las Olas Riverfront in 2011.

Two weeks later they closed another deal in Pompano Beach for two projects. One is a 2-acre beachfront twenty-seven-storey tower with ninety-two high-end condos, lush gardens and two swimming pools overlooking the ocean. The other is the Broadstone Oceanside, with 204 apartments and seven two-storeyed homes.

From 2010 till today, Dev and Bill have invested in more than ten properties. They opportunistically bought real estate from 2011 to 2014, buying assets that nobody wanted. While they waited for the markets to bounce back, Dev looked out for new projects. That has always been his forte.

By 2011, they started selling apartments at the Gale (which will be ready in 2018). After that, Dev moved south towards Trion Dania Beach, where the company closed in on a site that has been approved for an eight-storeyed apartment project featuring 286 units and 13,000 sq. ft of retail, which will be completed in 2019.

Dev closed a major deal in 2016—the Flagler Village Hotel ($1.9 million) with 202 rooms, which combined the Hilton brands of Tru and Home2 Suites. They partnered with Coral Gables–based Driftwood Hospitality for it and expect it to be completed in early 2019. A lot of thought went into this one as the new Bright line Station is being built right there, and the high-speed train service will finally run from Miami to Orlando in mid-2017. The second major deal was an apartment project, Flagler Village Apartments.

For the Riverfront property, Dev and Bill are planning a large two-phase mixed-use multi-family project on New River in the heart of Fort Lauderdale. It will have two towers of forty-two and forty-six storeys, respectively, 1214 units and 40,000 sq. ft of retail.

Modera Plantation is one property on which they will break ground in 2017 to build a five-storeyed, 250-unit mid-rise apartment in the Midtown Business District in Plantation. They also have Paramount Fort Lauderdale Beach on their hands, an eighteen-storeyed tower with ninety-five luxury condos on Fort Lauderdale Beach offering the privacy and exclusivity of a private residence, set to be completed in 2017.

Dev finds the finance side of his business more than interesting and easy, of course, since Credit Suisse prepared him for it. Everything after that has been about development, and that has given rise to his entrepreneurial side. He has adapted himself, evaluating situations along the way. In the US, because a lot of financing is available, along with insurance and risk, lenders and even investors prefer to engage a third party for construction. Typically, banks fund 50–60 per cent of the total project, and the rest comes from the partners. Since it takes so many years to actually see a project through, one has to be capital-rich to make it, or, as Dev says, one can make it the way his parents did, putting all their money back into the business as they made it. They didn't have the luxury to enjoy the money.

Today, even if the brothers are involved in separate projects individually, they are partners on all projects in spirit. Whether they have others on the deal or not, they are always on the same side. When they do have other partners, they are usually limited partners or investors. The two brothers make sure that they are always the developers, the sponsors, doing the principal work. Everything depends on the size of the deal, how much they have going on at the time and their capacity or desire to do more. The family has some noncore businesses too, such as investments in a window company and a brewery, Rock Brothers Brewery.

Today the Motwanis definitely have the ability to scale up better. They have moved from a small business to a hugely successful one. But with their upbringing, Nitin and Dev are still as involved as ever. Dev still rolls up his sleeves, is present at all the hearings, architect and commissioner's meetings. Ramola taught them to be one with the community and always maintain their sense of responsibility.

Civic Life

The Motwani family sponsors one or two charitable events every month. Dev plays an active role in the south Florida community, through his involvement with numerous charities and business organizations. He currently serves on the board of directors to the Broward Center for the Performing Arts Foundation, Broward College Foundation Board, Fort

Lauderdale's Historical and Economic Development Advisory Board, and Crockett Foundation.

He was recently appointed to the Orange Bowl Host Committee. The Motwani family also co-founded the Laughing Out Loud fundraiser, which raised over $1,70,000 for the charity for the benefit of the Scleroderma Foundation. Dev has also been named by *South Florida Business Journal* as the Ultimate CEO. The family recently received the honour of a star on the Fort Lauderdale Beach Walk of Fame.

Personal Life

Ramola's sons understand that she sacrificed a lot for them, probably never indulging herself, as she put them in good schools and provided the best for them. They got to actually enjoy life and experience things first-hand. Now they have turned that around, and both sons indulge her with their time and experiences, making sure she has the best of everything. The one thing she enjoys and asks for are annual holidays with the family. Dev is thrilled these days that his mother has found a little niche for herself in non-profit organizations and is helping her community.

Going to Duke University gave Dev and Nitin a lot of exposure, while the travel gave them more confidence. On graduating, Nitin was valedictorian while Dev was salutatorian. Both had excellent scores and the drive to perform. Speaking of his mother and how it is to work with somebody who is so dynamic, Dev says that by the time he came to the fore, she had become a lot calmer since Nitin had already come in and taken over some of the business. All three of them still take decisions collectively and run most things by Ramola, as her inputs are very important. It did take Dev time to be on top of the local market, since even though he grew up there he had been away for ten years. From a business point of view he is happy that his mother is still active in the community, because when projects are being built, one has to be involved and engaged. Together, he and Ramola have also managed to bring back the Fort Lauderdale Air Show on the beach successfully, increasing the number of people visiting the city and county.

Dev enjoys outdoor sports, loves playing tennis and attending sporting events. Work and family go hand-in-hand for him. Scuba diving is a favourite pastime and so is spending time with his nephews. Dev often travels abroad to get different perspectives on Fort Lauderdale and its development.

Today, Dev Motwani is a dealmaker, investor and visionary for the neighbourhood where he and his older brother, Nitin, once rode their bikes as children. He proudly wears the hat of president of Merrimac Ventures. He is also the founder and managing partner of Ramesh Properties, a distressed real estate investment fund focused on opportunistic investments in residential and commercial development sites throughout south Florida.

Patrick Murphy—Congressman

Patrick Murphy is a Democrat who campaigned with Hillary Clinton in 2016. From an illustrious Irish family in the construction business, he was a certified public accountant (CPA) who went into his family business in 2010, working as a day labourer and also in many departments of the business.

Later, Patrick went to Haiti to help with an oil spill. That opened his eyes to the possibilities in the government, and he decided to run so that he could make a difference. Patrick was in Congress for four years, representing the Palm Beach area of Florida, before he decided to run for the US Senate. He thought he had picked a winner in Hillary, but Trump won Florida. Now back in the family business, he dreams about running again.

Patrick has had a great association with the Motwani family. They supported him throughout his campaign with events and fundraisers and are now associated with him through their construction business. The trust factor is mutual, and Patrick says he would sooner shake hands with them than with anybody else along the coast.

He still remembers the huge dinner Ramola threw for his fundraiser in 2015 at her house while he was campaigning for Congress. She had people from all over the United States in donations. She was also there to share the lows when he lost.

The Motwanis Today

Nitin and Dev have always been very close. Despite being very different people, they share the same principles. Dev, in Nitin's opinion, is very much like his father, more of a risk taker, whereas he is a lot calmer.

The brothers share a deep family bond and speak several times a day. They have great admiration and respect for their mother, Ramola, and consider her an amazing resource who has taught them perseverance, patience and a positive attitude. Following in her footsteps, they both have numerous civic involvements. They have had their chance to put Fort

Lauderdale on the map by getting great activity back on the beach. For the Motwanis, it has been a thirty-year journey that has brought all this together.

Ramola is elated that her sons are carrying on the tradition that Bob and she had started. She says, 'There is nothing more fulfilling, more rewarding, as a parent than to see your legacy continue in your own lifetime.'

Harish Fabiani

The Family Tree

Motiram, married to Rajini

Kamal, married to Rachna

Harish, married to Roopa

Navin, married to Sonam

Kajal

Sonali

Simran

Introduction

Sindhis have always been known for their import/export expertise, since that is what they have done for centuries. Their modus operandi was to shift with their relatives, one by one, to different places all over the world, in order to enable the success of the whole family. This is also Harish Fabiani's story. Harish left the country in 1983 with an engineering degree. His older brother, Kamal, and he ran a successful electronics business and later ventured into real estate in Spain, as that activity was lucrative at the time.

Today, Harish is the chairman of the Madrid-headquartered $2 billion Americorp Group, which, through its private and public equity arms, owns financial interests in diverse businesses in the fields of technology, media, real estate and other sectors in the European Union (EU) and in India. Harish has founded and managed India Land Properties, a real estate company in India that develops IT parks, special economic zones (SEZs) and industrial parks in Chennai, Coimbatore and Pune. Harish has invested in and mentored many other entrepreneurs.

Harish distanced himself from the electronics business in Spain at its peak, as he understood that the world was changing with the advent of the Internet. He then travelled to Europe and America with his advisors, researching those markets. He wanted to diversify from his old business as he was intensely keen on investing in technology. In the meantime, the Indian market too was ready for the Internet explosion. Harish became one of the largest individual venture capital (VC) investors in India in media, telecom, fibre optics, telecom infrastructure, ISPs and other Internet-related businesses. He also became one of the country's first individual angel investors, with his $2 million investment in Indiabulls, along with Lakshmi Mittal, who invested $1 million in the same company. He is well-known as the pioneer of private equity financing in India.

One of my meetings with Harish was on his Bombardier Global 5000—his corporate jet, which reduces his travel time. This is the place where many a deal for his group has been cut. Equipped with a fully operating office, with telephones, large-screen televisions, faxes and computers, this is the place where Harish spends a lot of his time, attending to his various businesses.

He walks in tall and dapper, and in a very amiable mood, ready to take on the day and the matters at hand. He comfortably converses with his crew in Spanish, and after he is settled in, the jet takes off so smoothly that I have to look out to see if we are really up in the air. I watch him closely as he finishes his discussions with his colleagues.

When he started out, Harish invested $300 million in India. The media was quick to discover him then. Soon after, in 2003, he graced the cover of *Sindhian*, a prominent community magazine, acquiring a celebrity status and credibility. He was at one time the largest NRI investor in the country. Harish believes that India will be among the biggest players in the technology space in the years to come. Today, his companies invest in software, technology, media, telecom and real estate.

Harish's Bhaiband (a sub-community or caste) parents, Motiram, who is eighty-eight now, and Rajini Fabiani (who passed away) had their roots in Pakistan. They moved later to Baroda, and from there to Jaipur and consequently to Delhi. Today, Motiram's home is in Madrid, Spain. Talking about the family name, Fabiani, he recounts that the whole *bradri* (family) sat down one day in 1930 and decided they would choose from the following names—Lalvani, Purswani and Fabiani. Their uncle (Jhangimal) decided that Fabiani would suit them best, since their great-grandfather's name was Fabiomal. However, some relatives adopted the name Purswani.

Motiram Fabiani played an active part in the upbringing of both his children, Kamal and Harish. He believes that children should never be forced to do anything, allowed to explore the world for themselves and learn from making their own mistakes. Harish says Kamal and he were never restricted from actually following their hearts, whether it was to scale a mountain top or to just playfully pass their time.

They had a happy childhood in New Delhi. They were familiar with Jaipur too, as Harish and Kamal's mother hailed from there. Harish was analytical, even as a youngster, possessing a sharp intellect. Motiram recalls a Singapore visit the family made, when Harish had to take leave from school for three months. He was in high school then. In spite of this time away from studies, Harish passed the annual exam with flying colours.

Harish was born in 1962 in Patel Nagar. The family later moved to Rajouri Garden, along with Harish's chacha's family. Nine family members lived in a two-bedroom space in the early 1970s. Harish's upbringing in New Delhi was that of a typical child in a middle-class family. Kamal and Harish grew up in a warm atmosphere where there was emphasis on frugality and humility.

Harish's mother obviously had a very important role to play in his life. He remembers that even though they were from a middle-class family with limited resources, Rajini managed to fulfil all their needs. A BA graduate, she was a classy and elegant homemaker, who believed in simple living. She found the time to take care of the boys' education, taught them their morals and manners, and had enough foresight to insist that they be trained in the ways of the world so they could be independent individuals. She had them learn typing, basic cooking and sewing.

Harish has an early memory of Rajini bringing up the topic of how pilots made a lot of money, and so Harish's impulsive ambition at age eight was to become a pilot. It was an idea that did not leave him. Harish eventually got himself a flying licence, but he never quite became a commercial pilot because he was on his way to becoming an electronics engineer.

Harish attended Pusa Polytechnic after high school. He found himself studying electronics engineering, influenced by what his friends wanted to do. But his father made sure he was taught the basics of accounting while he was in the last year of high school, thinking he might need it for college. It was common for Sindhi fathers to make sure their sons learnt accounting and how things worked in business, teaching them how to create a balance sheet, a profit and loss account, etc.

In 1978, students joined college early, immediately after their graduation from school after tenth standard. Leaving school at fifteen and a half, as a result of having received a double promotion one year, suddenly seemed too early for Harish because he found the level of mathematics at college considerably higher and thus tough. To compete with that level of mathematics, which was required for engineering, Harish realized that he had to take a little help from his friend and neighbour, Hansraj. Turning his act around in three years, Harish finally received his engineering diploma with a distinction. Harish realized early in life that being carefree was hugely different from being careless. College life taught him to take his responsibilities seriously.

Post college, he acquired his first job as an electronics engineer in Delhi itself, working for Motwane Private Limited of Chicago Radio fame. It was a company that produced electronic multi-metres, amplifiers and other audio electronic equipment. Harish was instrumental in bidding for the tender for supplying audio equipment for the 1982 Asian Games at the National Stadium in Delhi, along with his boss Kiran Motwane. That year, theirs was the only Indian company that was awarded the tender, as all the other stadiums had given theirs to multinational companies.

In the 1960s, Harish's favourite chacha, a proper Sindhworki, moved away to work in Nigeria with the

Kishinchand Chellaram family. In the 1970s, this chacha shifted to Spain to work for another company. He ensured that all the sons in the family moved from Delhi to Spain for work, even though their salaries were nothing to write home about. This was typical of Sindhi families, with one relative informing his/her kin about job opportunities. Harish's older brother, Kamal, also joined his chacha's family in Spain, starting his career there in 1976 as a salesman in the family shop.

In 1981, when Harish was working with Chicago Radio, his maternal uncle asked him to pack his bags for Hong Kong. Harish left at two days' notice. His uncle and he started a company called Euro East Enterprises. Harish was barely nineteen and fresh out of college, with only six months' work experience. In 1983, his uncle resigned from the company and Harish could not acquire an extension for his visa. He feels that was his destiny, because he was soon on his way to Spain to join his brother, Kamal.

Motiram describes Harish's qualities with much warmth and candour, calling him a far-sighted businessman who knows how to take decisions without faltering. He talks about how Harish is a man of his word, doing the right thing at the right time. A little laugh gives away the fact that he feels Harish has taken after his mother, not only in his good looks but also in intelligence. He adds that luck has indeed favoured his younger son's life decisions.

Setting Up in Spain

Kamal returned to Madrid after his wedding in May 1983 and started his own company, Star Electronics. All imports into Spain came from Hong Kong in those days, since China was still not in the picture. By November, Harish was all set to join Kamal. He had just turned twenty-one. Since he knew no Spanish, his first task was to take language classes.

The brothers were young and eager to earn their money, and used their enthusiasm to further their business. Soon they became a force to deal with, despite being the newest kids on the block, up against some really old companies.

The boys did not take any money from their family, but used their Hong Kong office as a back-up and retained a smallish set-up for their work in Spain. They increased their imports and sold to wholesalers in Spain, and sometimes even to the big retailers. Their volumes matched their capital. Their imports were videotapes, audiotapes, adaptors, radios, portable audio-cassette players, two-in-one audio players, etc. The first year brought them a considerable profit ($100,000) as they did excellent business during the Christmas season. They were most definitely getting a feel of the trade. The fact that Spain was highly underserved and the markets were not well penetrated yet, since the Spaniards as a whole were restricted from doing import business, also contributed to their success.

General Franco (1936–1975) had made sure that Spain remained under dictatorship for a very long time. Only after his death did democracy free up matters for the Spaniards. He retarded the country's growth, making it fall behind other European countries. Spain felt like a virgin territory for business in imports and electronics. Finally, the king of Spain decided to do away with monarchical rule and installed a parliament in 1976.

The Fabiani brothers prospered, as did Spain side by side. There was enough business for everyone. Six months after setting up, in January 1984, one of the people the Fabianis worked with absconded, taking money worth $250,000. It was a truly dismal time for them, as they realized they could not do anything about it. As they had already lost everything they had made, they had nothing to do but to console themselves with the belief that god helps those who help themselves. They started all over again, and through the year strived to cover their losses. Their hard work paid off by the next year, resulting in remarkable volumes and healthy profits.

Their hard-earned success saw the brothers move from their small apartment to a massive villa (35,000 sq. ft) in a really posh neighbourhood. Of course, they did not have the ready capital to invest in such a big property. They put down only 20 per cent of the cost, borrowing 80 per cent from the bank. Back in 1984–1985 it cost them $550,000, but since their monies were good and growing, they easily paid off the bank in two to three years' time. Their new home had fifteen rooms, tennis courts, two swimming pools, service apartments, gardens, party spaces, and the like. It was nothing like any other Sindhi family had ever seen in Spain. That started a whole new movement in the community, bringing more Sindhis into the same locality.

Kamal and Harish's parents moved to Spain in 1984 to be with them. Motiram, with his wisdom and experience, took over the finances. He became the backbone of the company, making sure that the accounts were well-managed and controlled. The business boomed, as it became even more sound under their father's good guidance. It was only then that the young men splurged and bought their Mercedes and Porsches. They had worked hard but they had also bided their time before they partied. At twenty-two, Harish was the most eligible 'catch' in the Sindhi community.

For the Fabiani brothers, work always took precedence over everything else. They were now growing their market with goods from Japan and the US too, importing brands such as Pioneer and Panasonic, along with generic music systems, telephones, wireless telephones, etc. Their business was definitely galloping ahead faster than the rest of the market. At the time, very few had created the growth they had. Capital-wise, they were very strong and were able to handle more volumes. Over the years, they introduced more branded items into their electronics range.

From 1984, the business remained stable for another three or four years, but in 1988, a large trader who used to buy a lot of merchandise from many importers, including the Fabiani brothers, created a stir. The brothers heard a vague rumour that he was going to default on payments worth $40 million owed to people across the market, including themselves, and was liquidating some of his merchandise in order to flee the situation. Thirty years ago, $40 million was a large amount. The trader owed the brothers $2 million. Time was of the essence, as it was Christmastime and all sales were at a high. The Fabiani credit in the market was at its highest, and the situation looked pretty grim. If the man planned to skip off by 5 January, the brothers would feel the tremors by February end. But they were sitting on a secret, and seizing the opportunity, they confronted the trader and managed to settle the matter. They also sidestepped part of the disaster by accepting his house worth over $1 million and retrieving some of their products from him.

In the interim, they also got the names of their other clients whom the trader dealt with and squared off accounts with them too, thus reducing their risk in the market. Fast thinking and smart planning saved the day for the brothers. Harish was always the proverbial sharp Sindhi businessman. All their other competitors were badly hit, and that created a domino effect, weakening the whole market. Motiram at this time warned them to go slow, but Harish, the strategist, had other plans. He wanted to be even more aggressive in the market because his Sindhi mind realized that they were in the strongest position to spread their wings. Harish expanded the business. This decision sent the Fabianis into the top bracket of the market.

To date, Harish lives by the Spanish proverb: Ninety-nine gram of hard work and one gram of luck is needed for success. He has also always believed that it is not necessary that the person who works the longest can produce the best results. The brothers knew long days of work in the early years of their life in Spain, but nothing stopped Harish from striving even more. He always kept his goals in sight.

In 1990–91, the Fabianis moved into a new office space. They had grown so much that they built their own building, Surya, to house all their staff and accommodate the larger requirements of their business. They had the smaller office space lying free, and Motiram felt that since there was no place for Hindu worship in Madrid, they should dedicate that space to the Hindu community and build a temple there.

Harilela Family

Naroomal and Devi Bai

The Harilela brothers—George, Hari, Peter, Bob, Gary and Mohan

Holiday Inn Golden Mile Hong Kong

Holiday Inn Bangkok

Harilela Mansion, Hong Kong

Gary and his family

David with his family

Merrimac Ventures

Ramola with Dev, Nitin, Anshu and her grandchildren, Arin and Shaan, at their residence in Fort Lauderdale

Ramesh, Ramola, Nitin and Dev

With Hillary Clinton

Ramola and Dev with the Dalai Lama

Four Seasons, Fort Lauderdale

Gale Residences, Fort Lauderdale

Miami Worldcenter

Paramount Residences, Florida

Harish Fabiani

Harish Fabiani at his office in Mumbai

Harish with his father, Motiram

Harish with his wife and daughters, waiting to get on to their private jet

Harish with Dada Vaswani

With famous artist Raza on his birthday in 2015

Harish, Kamal and their parents with Sri Sri Ravi Shankar

With the president of Babson College, Kerry Healey

Harish with King Juan Carlos and Queen Sophia

With Donald Trump at the launch of Trump Tower in Mumbai in 2015

The iconic wave building in Chennai by the famous architect Zaha Hadid

India Land and KGISL Parks in Coimbatore

Lakhi Group

Pushpa Lakhi

Vishindas Holaram

Motiram Lakhi, Girdharilal Lakhi, Dilip Kumar Lakhi,
Prakash Lakhi and Deepak Lakhi

(From left to right) Amit Bakshi (younger son-in-law), Prerna Bakshi (younger daughter), Dilip, Karuna D. Lakhi (wife), Kaira Lakhi (daughter-in-law), Chirag D. Lakhi (son), Krsna Kalra (elder daughter), Suraj Kalra (elder son-in-law) and granddaughter Nanndika Kalra

Dilip and son, Chirag, with PM Modi

Dilip with Pratibha Patil

Dilip receiving an award from Vardha Shine

Dilip receiving a lifetime achievement award from Gems and Jewellery Export Promotion Council

Embassy Group

Jitu at the Embassy Lake Terraces project site

At the 2013 NDTV Property Awards, where Embassy Manyata Business Park won an award

Jitu with his favourite horse

(From left to right) Karan (son), Natalie (daughter), Jitu, Lina (wife), Neel (son) and Aditya (son) on Jitu's fiftieth birthday

(From left to right) Karan, Lina, Raj (mother), Motiram (father), Neel and Jitu

Inauguration of Stonehill Government Higher Secondary School. Jitu with Vishweshwar Hegde Kageri, the then minister of primary and secondary education

(From left to right) Kaushik Vardharajan, Guy Phillips, Jitu Virwani, Sartaj Singh and Michael Holland

Jitu with Karan, who heads the WeWork project

The WeWork building in Mumbai

Embassy Golf Links
Business Park

Embassy Lake Terraces

Hence the community got its own temple, a hall for religious ceremonies and *bhojan*, and a library for religious books. The family has deep-rooted faith in the Hindu religion. Motiram is also an RSS supporter and used to head a *shakha* in Hyderabad once. He is proud that Harish is a successful human being who has seen very good days and is glad that he continues to invest in spirituality and philanthropy in good measure, as he rightfully should give back to the world that has given him so much.

Their hard work made them the No. 1 electronics traders in Spain. They were now working even harder to bring in the bigger and better brands, as there appeared to be a massive opportunity for growth. They imported more and stocked more, got larger warehouses and employed more people. Strategies that definitely worked in their favour.

Personal Life

In 1989, Harish was the most eligible bachelor in the Sindhi community, with a lovely home, cars and a successful business. By now his family was getting restless about his single status and insisted on his engagement to a family friend's daughter. Being young and an obliging son, he complied. However, it didn't quite work out to Harish's liking, so he braved the winds and personally met the girl's family to call it off. That is exactly who Harish is—he likes to tackle all his problems himself.

Later, in 1990, he married Roopa Manghnani, whom he had been seeing in Madrid after his engagement broke. They were engaged on an auspicious day selected by the families, and they married on Shivratri the same year.

Roopa had met Harish while she was directing a play for the Diwali ball in Madrid a year and a half before they got married. Even during those early days she appreciated his strength of character as he vied for her attention. However, she made all the rules on where and when he would attend practice sessions. Initially they did not quite hit it off; they often had arguments as their very different personalities clashed. But love soon won over.

Harish had broken off the earlier engagement because he wanted to stay true to his heart. He wanted to spend time with Roopa and acted on his feelings. But by then Roopa had already left for India because she did not want to be one of the many pining for the most eligible catch in town. Harish pursued her after he broke off the engagement, and they finally tied the knot with their parents' blessings. Roopa says that once Harish makes up his mind, there is little anyone can do to stop him.

Having completed her master's degree in industrial psychology from Mumbai, Roopa thought she would pursue a career in Spain, but that did not happen as the joint Sindhi family system did not encourage women in the workplace. When it comes to family values and culture, Harish believes in the upkeep of old traditions, to the extent that his wife is not allowed to call him by his name. He is a modern man in the world of business, but when it concerns his family and children, he is orthodox to a fault. He even preferred to have his children grow up in India.

Very much a family man, Harish makes it a point to talk to his father as often as he can, from wherever he is in the world. In the early 2000s, when his mother was still alive, he chartered a yacht and took his whole family for a fifteen-day cruise on the Mediterranean.

Expanding the Business

By 1990, the Fabiani brothers had expanded exports to Germany, France, Holland, Switzerland and England. At that time Kamal and Harish were working together, one managing sales and the other the business side. Kamal turned out to be quite the salesperson; people thought he could even sell ice to an Eskimo. He was a good businessman, with an eye for the right pricing, and he could very easily procure the right merchandise. People loved doing business with him because they trusted him. He clearly understood a product's market and its requirements. His people skills took him far, and he created lasting relationships for the company. So while Harish could manage the product deals, personally dealing with suppliers like Panasonic, Aiwa and Sanyo, Kamal was instrumental in improving sales. This combination of skills helped them grow manifold and increased their sales volumes.

Malls came into existence in the 1990s. Harish joined the bandwagon and started supplying to these 'hypermarkets', in spite of his margins being severely hit. He realized this was the beginning of the end for middlemen like him. Harish had a foreboding of things to come, which he felt in the pit of his stomach. He questioned the longevity of a business like his, in spite of it being at the top of the industry.

In 1995, he realized that he could not go on doing the business he was doing and gave himself five years' time to regroup. He felt the train that he was on, though moving

ahead powerfully, was heading towards a dead end. He
realized that he would have to get off the train sooner than
later and get on to another train headed towards something
that would last him a lifetime. Harish saw the paradigm shift
coming, and it proved to be the game changer in his life. He
needed to diversify into something that would have a longer
business run. At that time, he never thought he would come
to India.

Though Harish had begun to make long-term plans, the
year 1996 turned out to be an even bigger one than 1995.
Turnovers soared, land banks grew, and at thirty-three he felt
he had the world in his palm. But at the back of his mind he
knew he was headed for change. So Harish started investing
in the US stock market and began to travel more extensively.
Around the same time, Harish visited India too. He would
visit every couple of years as was the norm for him.

Looking to India

Working in India at the time felt very difficult, considering
the number of hurdles one had to clear to reach one's goal.
But for Harish, many things were simpler because he was
a foreign investor, and the single most important thing he
needed was an FDI (Foreign Direct Investment) approval.
The better tax structure and some benefits were what
attracted most foreign investors to India. To date, however,
there are not many foreign investors. There are institutions
and funds—such as Fidelity Capital and Goldman Sachs.

By 1995, India had begun to look good in terms of
investment. Harish, on one of his trips, visited Bangalore
(now Bengaluru) along with a friend to earmark some prime

property. A true entrepreneur and man with a vision, Harish always looked for new investments, whether in ideas or real estate. He bought 5 or 6 acres of land (at Rs 20 lakh per acre) on the main highway from some villagers. He foresaw growth in that area. Working on his instincts, he paid them a certain amount to seal the deal, as a kind of advance against the total value agreed upon. He wrote down a few important details, such as the sellers' names, his name as the buyer, the cost of the land, the amount given in advance and the balance to be paid in three months' time on a soiled tissue paper since they were having chai at a roadside teashop while conducting the deal.

Harish took the sellers' signatures and put his down as well. He then went back to Spain. When he returned three months later, the owners refused to sell him their land at the earlier price agreed upon, telling him the price had gone up. Luckily, Harish had saved the piece of signed tissue paper and brought it to their notice. Harish almost triumphantly relates this story, saying it should be everyone's golden thumb rule to sign on something the very moment a transaction is agreed upon, even though one may be signing on just tissue paper.

Things finally worked out, and Harish paid just a little more than the agreed-upon amount to make the sellers happy. Since he came back fifteen days later than he intended to, he paid them an interest too. Harish talks about how he sold the same piece of land just last year for between Rs 12 and Rs 14 crore per acre. Holding on to the land for twenty years got him fifty times his investment, fetching him more returns than he would have got by building something on the land and selling it.

Investing in the stock markets came with a lot of learning for Harish, even though he was an engineer and could understand commerce too. He was definitely a quick learner, almost a natural, as he evaluated companies and scrips better than most people and understood the technology sector too. But not knowing much in 1996–1997, he dared to invest in the US, and realized after about six months that he had made a loss of a quarter of a million dollars on his first investment.

What seemed like a failure was the biggest lesson that Harish learned, as he was not the kind of man who would take something like that lying down. He promptly joined an executive education course (he was thirty-seven and the youngest in the course) in one of the best Spanish schools—the IESE Business School, ranked fourth in the world by the *Financial Times*. But the course was in Spanish, and though Harish understood and spoke colloquial Spanish, he still needed a dictionary at all times, since studying a technical subject in the language turned out to be an entirely different matter.

It was a six-month part-time course, basically meant for older business entrepreneurs who did not want to simply obtain an MBA but who needed to understand company operations, finance, human resources and decision-making. The course completely changed Harish's life and readied him for his various businesses.

India's Angel Investor

Harish Fabiani ended up being in India at the right time. He came to the country in 1997 to diversify from his business in Spain. Even though he continued to live in Spain, he was in touch with chosen investment bankers about the interests he could pursue in India, since they understood what he was looking for. On one of his trips, he came with his analyst to conduct due diligence on a company called Pentafour Software and Graphics in Chennai.

Harish then asked a Merrill Lynch software analyst to write a report on Pentafour Software. The analyst pronounced that the company's share price could quadruple. His analyst was of the opinion that there were only three or four companies in the whole world that had the same working capacities as Pentafour, to develop the products it did and be on a par with the best in the world. This company was really worth investing in. Over the fortnight, when Harish was in India talking business to the company, the stock price soared 10 per cent higher than what he had been promised.

The chairman of the company, Chandra Shekar, was hugely apologetic, but he said he would consider something a little different and offered Harish a completely new global depository receipt of $15 million. Speaking to his bank, Fabiani realized that he could only raise up to $7 million, but his bank offered to meet him on the balance. Harish agreed. But a few days later the bank bailed out and said they could only come up with $4 million. Now Harish was in a bind, but still kept his word and gave the company the $11 million tranche, closing the deal with a 20 per cent stake in it.

Harish invested in Pentafour Software in April 1997. He noticed many problems in the company, such as basic corporate governance and non-transparency issues. He communicated this to the company, suggesting major changes, such as having on board any one of the top four audit companies. He absolutely insisted on the company being more accountable and trustworthy, and declaring results every quarter. He told them their transparency would get them more credibility.

Within two quarters of Harish buying the 20 per cent stake, the company's image improved. Progress in the IT sector added to this, leading to a 100 per cent increase in the company's stock price that year. The stock was re-rated, and Harish exited his original investment with a 500 per cent return. Having invested $11 million, he was now sitting on $58 million, a year later, in September 1998. At the time of these investments in 1997–1998, Harish set up his India investment vehicle, called TransAtlantic Corporation.

Before 2000 (Y2k), everybody in the tech world was wary of problems that might be caused in computers because of the change of 00 in the date. The world over, big companies had to hire the cheapest labour in the globe to tackle that line-by-line change that had to be made in coding. India at the time got the most work from the US and other countries. Export of labour became the norm in India, which simply meant expansion for businesses in India.

Harish felt India had the most promising potential and strongly believed even at that time that India would at some point become one of the biggest technology hubs in the world. For him it made sense to train and send people to India to tap the best potential there and avail the economic advantage in terms of labour costs.

With the experience he had gathered from a software company he had in the US, Harish now understood the IT sector even better than he did earlier. This spurred him to invest in more companies in that sector in India. Understanding the Indian economy well, more so because he was Indian, he made the right decisions.

Within a short period of time another company, Silverline, approached Harish. This time Fabiani sent an analyst from Goldman Sachs to evaluate the company. For him, such a review was a very important practice. Since the company had Indian and US operations, it had to be reviewed carefully. Silverline was a US company that owned an Indian entity, and the promoter at the time wanted to list the US company on Nasdaq in America. This did not make sense to the analyst since it would not create much value. So they suggested to the company to do the listing the other way round—the Indian company gets listed and owns the American entity—for better valuation. In 2000, when the company got listed on Nasdaq, Harish's investment of $30 million became $300 million within a year. With this huge appreciation, he sold about 25 per cent of his holding in the company.

Harish started to invest in many other software companies and simultaneously looked for other private equity candidates too. He was now more open to looking at start-ups. His presence in the US and in India simultaneously was important for his work. Harish found so much more innovation on American shores. He understood and was very enamoured by the strides technology was taking, understanding well that software would remain the backbone of the industry. All that drove him to make place for operations in the US in the sector.

In 1999, Fabiani started a $10 million operation in the US called Ecom Server. He created a space in Princeton

(New Jersey), getting on board three other founding partners—Raj Salgam, Nixon Patel and Rakesh Patel—who were experts in the field and lived there. Ecom Server was a software company dealing with e-commerce, providing solutions for B2B e-commerce and CRM. It was a growing sector, tackling new technology and terminology, and involved the higher end of software development.

Harish loved that part of it because of his past experience with software companies. Indian companies had been doing the same work, but they were doing lower-end work. US companies, he found, had an edge over them because they were closer to the client and could fulfil their requirements with the latest technologies and software. Setting up a company in the US was an expensive proposition, but Harish made sure the back office was set up in Hyderabad. This proved to be Harish's learning curve for the Indian operations that were to follow. Ecom Server did fairly well, and by early 2002 Harish sold it to another US company for a reasonable profit.

Americorp Ventures Ltd (2000)

All the travel to and from America and running a business there with a back office in India taught Harish more about how to conduct business in India.

Now, having decided to invest in the software, media and tech sectors in India, Harish felt the need to have the best deals flow towards him first, for which he strategically looked for companies to buy stakes in or invest in their stocks. With this in mind, he took a stake in Edelweiss Capital in 1998, as they were one of the largest deal-sourcing companies at the time in the technology space.

Media Investments

TV18 caught Harish's interest when he heard that they were setting up CNBC in India. He invested Rs 18.07 crore in it. He was interested in acquiring stock in more media companies in India, so he invested Rs 40 crore in Harish Thawani's Nimbus Communications. In hindsight, he regrets ever considering it, calling it his worst investment and the operations a gross mismanagement of a beautiful company. Fabiani said Thawani resorted to fighting instead of amicably settling issues. There were so many delays that the company never went on to the IPO stage. The company still exists, but the courts have fined it for breaking its contracts with the Board of Control for Cricket in India. Harish has since written off his money in Nimbus.

Harish invested Rs 16.47 crore for a 20 per cent equity stake in a Mumbai-based media television software company, Popular Entertainment Network (widely known as PEN). It owned the rights to a large number of Bollywood movies and also had the right to extend them to TV channels to air the films. PEN was the same company that acquired the rights to the super-hit film *Kaho Na Pyaar Hai,* starring Hrithik Roshan, for about Rs 1.25 crore. But corrective valuations along the years in music rights and movie libraries caused the final collapse of the company. It never reached the IPO stage and ended up being a loss-making investment for Fabiani.

In 1999, Cal Tiger (Patriot Automation Projects Private Limited) was brought to Harish by Edelweiss Capital. The company, an Internet service provider, aimed to offer free Internet for all. That system needed a modem and a dial-up service on the phone, which then connected to a gateway etc.

It was, of course, a model copied from countries such as the US. Fabiani loved the idea and invested Rs 32 crore in it. Within a year and a half, the company consumed all the money before folding up.

In 2000, Harish invested in a company called C Bay. It wanted to do medical scripts for US doctors. The business took off phenomenally because doctors found it tedious and time consuming to write histories of their patients. With C Bay, they merely made audio recordings of medical histories and emailed them to offices in India to be rewritten, coded correctly and sent back by email.

This way, doctors' offices had files containing complete information on their patients. It was a beautiful model, because it saved the doctors the money they would have paid to employees in the US. Fabiani had put in $1 million in the company, and Franklin Templeton another $1 million. It was acquired by an American company and got listed in the US. It is still in business today. It was a good investment, as Harish made a profit when he exited a few years ago.

Similarly, Jalwa.com was a business Harish understood and liked, as it was founded to create digital prints of old movies. He invested $1 million because the promoters were young, had great ideas, and had as one of their co-directors, Amitabh Bachchan. But somehow the company did not survive. Maybe it was too early and the idea was before its time, but companies with similar concepts are doing pretty well today.

Soon after this, Fabiani invested in a TV channel co-owned by Raji Menon, who was the original promoter of Asianet TV. The channel was leading in Kerala, their biggest market being the Middle East. Millions of Keralites watched

Asianet for local news, shows, movies, etc. Asianet proved that they had the audience and the demand. Harish invested Rs 15 crore for a 10 per cent stake in the company in 2000 and exited making ten times the amount he invested after about twelve years.

The Edelweiss Group

The Edelweiss Group is one of India's leading financial services conglomerates. After exchanging notes with Rashesh Shah, who is the chairman and CEO of the group and also co-founder of Edelweiss Financial Services Ltd with Venkat Ramaswamy, one realizes that they have had a run of more than twenty-five years in the financial sector in India. Today the company has a big asset base and has five businesses—capital markets, asset management, credit, commodities and insurance.

Rashesh remembers hearing about a big investor who was coming down from Spain, looking for investment opportunities. Harish's reputation of being a smart investor preceded his visit. In 1998, Rashesh got to meet the man himself, when Harish showed interest in signing on Edelweiss to acquire deals for him.

Harish was impressed with Edelweiss. He thought the company consisted of very good professionals, and that they could easily become a reputed investment bank in India, especially because there were very few, and this company could compare with the best like DSP and Merrill Lynch, and Kotak Mahindra.

Later, Harish invested in Edelweiss itself, becoming the first outside investor in the company. The company was

five years old at this point, and until then had been fully
internally owned. But Harish's instincts were sharp and he
recognized their potential and seized the opportunity. He was
able to convince Rashesh that he would be a great investor in
their firm. His reasons were clear, he informed them that he
wanted a stake in the company because it was important for
a newcomer like him to have these kinds of companies in his
portfolio, so that other companies could take him seriously.
At the time, Harish invested Rs 4 crore in Edelweiss for a
10 per cent stake in the company.

Rashesh had no doubts about Harish, seeing that he
had already made some interesting and extremely intelligent
choices in the market, such as TV18 and some technology
companies. Harish was equally savvy about identifying the
right managerial teams. Rashesh remembers how, when TV18
was just about to launch its IPO and people were pegging its
stock value at Rs 100, an investor was offloading a block of
them at Rs 180 apiece. Harish calmly walked in and agreed to
buy at that price, closing the deal at the same rate without any
haggling. That shocked Rashesh, as he thought Harish would
bargain. Three months down the line, when the company's
IPO was done and it got listed, the shares rocketed to Rs 1,800
each. Harish had made himself ten times the money he had
put in just by recognizing a good company and seizing the
opportunity when it presented itself.

In Rashesh's opinion, Harish was one of the few investors
who had both a trading instinct and an investment instinct.
Usually people turn out to be either just traders, who are
interested only in the short term, or investors, who think only
long term. Harish is definitely a person whom Rashesh would
discuss market trends with and take honest advice from.

By the time Harish invested $35 million across ventures, he had seen some pretty great returns. All his friends told him to start a fund to which they could contribute to reap the benefits of his investment judgement. So he obliged them. But only part of the money in his fund belonged to his friends, and the rest was all his because he felt it was not the easiest thing to run a fund management company. It was registered in 2000 as a foreign venture capital fund in India.

All his investors benefited as the performance levels of the fund rose and the valuations of its investments increased. Harish made sure that he cashed out from half the companies so that he could use the same money to seed other businesses. Being in the finance, technology and software industries, Harish invested in fifteen companies in these areas. Only five reported losses. With another two or three, he got his money back, but the rest of them yielded amazing returns. When one has a portfolio, of this size, the law of averages definitely holds. Yet, when Harish returned his friends' monies, they made a return of six times their investment.

Incidentally, at around the same time that Harish was investing in those companies, HCL Technologies (Shiv Nadar's company) was coming out with its IPO. One of the analysts at ISEC, which was handling the IPO of HCL, went all the way to Madrid to make a beautiful presentation on the company to Harish, as he was one of the major angel investors in India. Gaurav Deepak's, twenty-four at that time, presentation was so good that Harish was absolutely floored. He told Deepak that any time he wanted to start a venture on his own, he (Harish) would back him. Six months later, Gaurav went back to Fabiani.

Avendus Advisors

Gaurav Deepak came across as an unassuming man at the meeting I had with him. From his humble and down-to-earth demeanour, one cannot tell how well this man has engineered his future since he met Harish Fabiani.

In the summer of 1999, ICCI's sister-unit, ISEC, which was a broking arm of ICCI, had taken on the work for the IPO of HCL Technologies. The main analyst on the project had excused himself to go on a holiday. Gaurav, who had never written a research report before, found himself not only writing it but also presenting it. The HCL head, Shiv Nadar, watched him present it and approved it.

Gaurav found himself meeting with Harish in Madrid. He was immediately awed by Harish's style and his home. They hit it off well, and the respect and regard each felt for the other was mutual. Harish offered Gaurav a job which he refused, since he was happy where he was. That was when Harish offered to back Gaurav in any venture he might start.

Six months later, Gaurav called him up. He wanted funding for his own start-up. There were three founding partners, and Harish had been offered a 33 per cent stake in the start-up. Harish immediately obliged, and invested Rs 1 crore, transferring a small amount that Gaurav had asked for to start with. Harish was very confident about Gaurav and did not ask any questions at all.

Initially, Gaurav's company, CoolStartups.com, helped Harish with some of his investments. After the dotcom bust, they changed their name to Avendus Advisors Pvt Ltd. Gaurav remembers Harish introducing them to his company in New York, Ecom Server. They did a phenomenal job with that mandate. But one of their biggest success stories was Indiabulls. Sameer Gehlaut was an IIT batchmate of Gaurav's partner, Kaushal Agarwal. Gaurav believed Sameer had a distinctive personality even in college, and is that person even today.

Sameer expressed a need for $3 million for his new start-up, and Avendus agreed to help him. Gaurav, in the meantime, met Rishi Khosla, who was working with the Mittals through a mutual friend. It was a really interesting time, when many young IIT graduates had big dreams and were realizing them at an amazing speed. Gaurav eventually got Rishi to meet Sameer, and Sameer found himself in a meeting with Laxmi Mittal's son, Aditya. Unfortunately, Aditya was interested in investing only $1 million, also only if the remaining $2 million was already available. Meanwhile, Gaurav also introduced Sameer to Harish Fabiani on the same trip. Harish led the investment with $2 million and cemented the deal by getting a 20 per cent stake in the company. All the other investors, including the Mittals, followed.

Avendus needed to first institutionalize the firm for longevity and needed to scale up. They did not want to end up running a boutique-type of business when they were in their forties. So in February 2016, Avendus made a deal with KKR (one of the largest private equity funds in the world) who gave them $100 million for a 51 per cent stake in the company. Avendus bought out some of the existing investors, and gave buyout options to some others (like Harish). But Gaurav and the other founding members decided to stay on. They felt as though they had an obligation towards the company and were the custodians of somebody else's wealth. They plan to further build the business over the next five years.

Today Avendus Advisors is the biggest investment banking company in India. In fact, it was the only one, along with Goldman Sachs, which was given the mandate to help sell Satyam Computers. The firm has seen a lot of ups and downs, but it has come out looking good. Harish sold part of his stake in Avendus when KKR acquired it, fetching a seventy-fold return on his investment.

Indiabulls

Walking into One Indiabulls Centre felt daunting. There was security everywhere. A private elevator took one directly to the top floor where everything exuded an air of importance. I stepped into the office of a very young, unassuming, well-known billionaire. It was a teak office with large sofas and offered a spectacular view of Lower Parel in Mumbai. Calm and well-spoken, Sameer Gehlaut did not fail to impress.

Sameer and his co-founders and partners, Rajiv Rattan and Saurabh Mittal, all from IIT Delhi, made it big with their online broking company, Indiabulls Financial Services Ltd, advancing with their ideas of property development and consumer finance. They had asked Mumbai-based Avendus Advisors to scout for angel investors for them. Harish clearly remembers his first meeting with the boys in a garage filled with computers. For them he was the big guy who worked with intuition and was known to smell money from a mile away, and who was extremely good at risk management.

The two investors that IBFSL can never forget are Harish Fabiani, who led the funding round with $2 million, and Lakshmi Mittal, who followed later, with $1 million. It was a great leap of faith for the investors as the boys were looking to be the Charles Schwabs of India in e-trading with their online brokerage. They wanted to replicate what had made a big splash in America. They had the right technological background and had developed in-house the software for transacting on stock markets. They were the first company to do so in India.

In 2004, Indiabulls went public. Sameer remarks that the company at the time of the Fabiani investment was valued at $10 million. The group has since moved into many different sectors. Today its market capitalization is close to $6 billion. Sameer is happy that they have turned out to be one of the top ten dividend-paying groups in India, all this within fifteen years of the company being set up.

Sameer agrees that it's not been completely smooth sailing; they have had to shut down some retail businesses. Harish has proved to be professionally sound, but one can also really count on him more as a friend now, as he is just a phone call away. For instance, when Sameer established his real estate development business in central London, he invited Harish to invest in that too. Together they also bought a stake in a bank there. Other than these international investments, Indiabulls is pretty much focused on its domestic businesses. Investors in the group have special rights but they don't get to be part of the management.

A reserved person usually, Sameer, forty-three, is all smiles when he says the reason for his success has been mere luck and not his intelligence. He adds that one is not even eligible for the race if one is not hardworking. When India was taking off, Indiabulls was at the right place at the right time. So was Harish, with his foresight.

Then came a twist in the story. The dotcom bust all over the world invariably left its trail even in India. Indiabulls was built as an online business. It had spent a lot of its capital on advertising and brand building. Sameer met with Harish to ask for more funds, which Harish flatly refused, saying they were going about it all wrong and he wouldn't oblige this time. At this point, Indiabulls was left with only limited funds. It shook Sameer to the very core as a deep fear now set in. He pulled up his socks immediately and curbed all unnecessary expenses.

Harish's refusal came from his expertise in dealing with US companies. He had to make sure his investee companies knew their limits. Once he invested, Harish left them to their own machinations and never tried to micromanage them, though he was always helpful. That has been his way of working in every deal. Sameer was smart, he changed his company's revenue model and turned things around. The group brought into existence twenty-seven brick-and-mortar offices all over India and switched to a physical presence, working even harder. Their smart move turned the business around.

Indiabulls also smartly added to its activities; from broking for its customers, it moved them to shares, then converted them into clientele for their home loans. This became the major revenue activity for the company—lending customers money for ten to twenty years to buy a home. Repayment in instalments was encouraged so that the company earned even more interest. Even though the banks were doing exactly the same thing, Indiabulls fed the glut at the time, since the demand for such loans was massive. Profits started to pour in slowly but surely.

In 2004, when Indiabulls issued an IPO, its share price opened at Rs 24 and jumped to Rs 80 in a short span of time. Harish sold some of his stake only when the share price shot past Rs 450. In 2005–06, the best time to deal in real estate, Indiabulls ventured into the business. Sameer emerged as the biggest bidder for mill land on which now stands One Indiabulls Centre. So Harish now had two companies, both doing well, and both separately listed. By 2007–08, Harish's investment was worth 200 times the original amount. At that time he sold 30–40 per cent of his holdings.

By 2006, Harish had also exited TV18 and Edelweiss.

The Topaz Fund

On his travels to the US in 2000, Harish was very active in investing in technology companies. He started a new tech fund, called Topaz Fund, out of New York. He chose a very qualified young fund manager, who was a graduate of Stern School (NYU). The fund grew by 40 per cent in the first forty days itself, posting record growth. Then came 9/11; there was mayhem on Wall Street and the ripples were felt all around the world. The crisis took Harish back to the US, where he found that his fund manager, Viraj Parekh, was suffering from depression, as was the whole of America. That prompted the closure of the fund.

Strategic Ventures

Singapore-based Atim Kabra got to know Harish in 2000 through common friends when he was at ABN AMRO Bank in New York City. Their dream was to start a private equity fund. At the time it was still the early days of private equity, and Atim was quick to share his hesitancy on account of this. Harish wanted to work with a professional, and offered Atim the job of managing his fund.

The ball was set rolling when Harish told Atim to look for some of his investments in India along with Rohit, who was Harish's private banker. Already, 70 per cent of the fund contribution was Harish's. Atim was then pretty clear that he would have to set up an independent entity to manage the investments. They had tremendous respect for each other and Atim had enough leeway to make his own decisions, despite the capital being Harish's.

So Strategic Ventures Fund Mauritius Ltd (SVFML) was set up as a private fund in New York in 2003. Atim started the fund along with Rohit, but soon found out that Rohit had other plans, so he ended up managing the money himself.

Atim invested for SVFML in EXL Services, which was amongst the earliest business process outsourcing companies. The deal made money, but by the time they exited they lost some parts of the gains. There were a few bombs in the portfolio, but Atim and Harish did go on to discover companies like Astra Microwave Products for $7 million, which went on to become India's largest listed defence electronics company in the private sector. When they exited after nine years, it was a mega success and their investment had appreciated fortyfold.

C Bay Systems, another of their investee companies, with Atim's help, went on to become the world's largest medical transcription company. This was a really interesting transaction, in Atim's opinion, because the stock was acquired in a different way, through multiple rounds of buying. The fund also bought secondary stock from other investors at a discounted price, and over time also picked up a 5 per cent stake in the company.

The interesting part thereafter was that their first investment in the company did not entitle them to further allotment of stock from the company, as they were the early investors. But as the valuations got higher they bought the stocks from the secondary market and were able to add to their holdings, at a lower cost. Over a period of time many investors exited the company. Harish and Atim were also able to help the company raise significant amounts of money from other investors. The company then went global, listing in the UK and the US; Harish and his company now exited as the company stood strong, making nearly five times their initial investment.

Similarly, in the case of Titagarh Wagons, they were the first to invest, and exited in various stages. As a result, their last exit was post the listing of the company, when other investors were just about putting their money into the company. Their role was to move out while their contribution lessened, letting other people come in and play their roles. Shilpa Medicare (an oncology-focused manufacturer in the pharma industry) was another such company that Harish and Atim invested in.

In 2016, Harish also bought a stake in Suryoday Small Finance Bank Ltd. An IPO of Tejas Investments, another company he invested in, also closed recently. His exit from the outfit after eight years fetched him 200 per cent returns.

Harish has always been open to investing in a wide spectrum of companies and industries. It is not very often that one finds investors who understand the life cycle of investments, but Harish has a wide portfolio to boast of. With fifteen investments in the listed space and many strategic ventures, the last twelve years have made for a good long run for them. They have had a good compounded annual rate of return of 22 per cent.

Spanish Ties

Harish's family moved to Mumbai in 2000 since he wanted his children to have an Indian upbringing. However, he was not happy with the quality of life that Mumbai afforded him, so he travelled between Spain and India. In Spain, his real estate development activity was doing well. Harish also had substantial holdings in banks in Europe, specifically in Spain and the UK, and in the US. He was one of the big shareholders of Banco Santander and BBVA.

Harish had always wanted Spain and India, two countries he absolutely loves, to have bilateral trade, and for himself to be in the middle of it all. Spain has always been very strong in the infrastructure and construction sectors. In 2007, when then prime minister, Zapatero, came to India on an official visit with many Spanish businessmen, Harish was in the group to see how India-Spain business ties could be widened. A formal delegation of thirty visited India, but didn't really get the attention they deserved, Harish thought, as there wasn't enough press coverage.

Zapatero did not get to meet any of the prominent ministers, though he was received in two formal receptions, and no major business was concluded either, in spite of his bringing a Spanish delegation along. But thankfully, today Spanish companies have entered the Indian business scene.

From that experience, Harish realized what was missing and worked on it in 2008 when he was instrumental in bringing the former prime minister of Spain, Jose Maria Aznar, to India. Aznar's word carries a lot of weight and he has been given the credit of bringing Spain to the forefront of the world stage. In the eight years of his governance, Spain grew the most. Being a fan, Harish was keen to bring him to India. A deep friendship arose between them. Aznar wanted to initiate communication with the top industrialists, businessmen and politicians in India in order to strengthen economic and political ties between the two countries.

Meetings were arranged in Mumbai ahead of time. Mukesh Ambani welcomed Aznar to India with a lavish dinner that included the big names of Mumbai, from Bollywood celebrities to sportsmen, businessmen and bankers. Harish made sure Aznar was also exposed to the culture of India.

India Land and Properties Private Ltd

Real estate had always been a passion for Harish. A forerunner in many areas, Harish started a company, Surya Investments, in 1988 to manage his assets and properties in Spain. It still does so to this day.

To test the waters, the company in 1988 used the extra swimming pools, tennis courts, party space, service apartments and gardens of the Fabiani residence to create four villas. Selling them fetched good returns, since the markets were strong post 1983, when Spain joined Europe and became a part of the world markets. The Fabianis ended up making more money than they had spent on buying the expensive house. This lucrative exercise egged on Harish to do more, and he knew that he would get into real estate in a big way one day.

In Spain, doing business was simpler than in India as corruption levels were very low. At certain levels influence could help marginally, but normally work was not hindered. If one was in the real estate business, one could easily finish one's work in record time with no complications. One could complete an entire project, with approvals, in two years' time.

For his Indian real estate acquisitions, Harish set up India Land. Through this company, he has developed 4 million sq. ft till date, comprising IT parks, IT SEZs, industrial parks, commercial property and other real estate in major Indian cities, such as Chennai, Coimbatore, Pune and Mumbai.

When an opportunity to invest in a 10-acre plot in Anna Nagar in Chennai beckoned, Harish remembered the good days of dealing with Ecom Server in Hyderabad, and realized that south India would prove to be a good base for his activities.

IT was the sector he clearly understood, so he seized the opportunity to develop 2.5 million sq. ft for a commercial IT park in Chennai in 2005. It was a sizeable first for an IT park, and this excited the developer in him since the projects in Spain were never this large. The Spanish population itself was only 45 million, and the requirements in that country in comparison with India's were minuscule.

Harish took on the project entirely on his own, without any partners, relying on just his knowledge of the sector and the expertise of his seniors in India Land in Tamil Nadu. The project, being an IT initiative and a foreign direct investment, seemed easier, with a lot of tax benefits. A few others, such as the Embassy Group and the Rahejas, had started similar projects a year or two before India Land. The software sector in India was growing exponentially and demand for space was huge. It was a time when not only companies like TCS and Infosys needed these IT parks, but also the BPOs that were coming up.

Started in 2005, Harish's India Land Tech Park has a leasable area of 2 million sq. ft, with amenities such as a food court, a childcare centre and a mini supermarket. Harish chose Zaha Hadid (the 2004 Pritzker laureate), an iconic businesswoman who passed away in 2016, to work on the project. Her partner, Patrick Schumacher, was actively involved, and they decided that the building would resemble a wave. Since the project was in India, they were flexible and charged a lower rate for their work. That is how India got its very own exclusive Zaha Hadid building.

Pune became the site of Harish's next venture in 2007—India Land Global Industrial Park in Hinjewadi. With a total developable area of 28 acres, its current key occupants are Walter (a unit of the Boryszew Group, Poland), Victaulic (USA), Spear Logistics (Honeywell Partners), Atlas Copco and Henkel.

Soon afterwards came the global financial collapse of 2008. The banking sector uses the most IT and BPO services, and the economic downturn resulted in a complete lull in demand for rentals. At the same time, Harish's company had invested in land in Coimbatore for another IT SEZ, a project more advanced than a tech park. But now the company was caught in the middle of a downslide, facing a massive crisis of sorts.

In all probability, it was because of the fabulous structure created by Zaha Hadid's company and the superior quality of infrastructure that attracted Royal Bank of Scotland to the first building in the tech park in 2008. And though India Land managed to sign on their anchor tenant, they found it difficult to get more renters. They had already built three sixteen-storey towers, with steel girders and glass panels lavishly fixed across their façade. But slowly, local companies started coming in. Today the park houses Kone Elevators, Reliance BPO, Covenant, Telebuy and Yes Bank, among the bigger names.

Chennai has always been Harish's favourite place to invest in. India Land acquired 400 acres in 2008–09, a forty-minute drive from the airport, to develop a township. Since there is an oversupply situation, India Land is going slow on the project. India Land's business model is focused on constructing and renting out. Harish's strategy is to not cash out on commercial rentals and sell residential properties as they do not bring in high rentals.

In 2010, India Land built an IT SEZ park, India Land KGiSL Tech Park, in Coimbatore. With a total development area of about 1.9 million sq. ft, this park already has tenants, such as Robert Bosch, Ugam Solutions, Aditi Technologies, Ebix Systems, M Model and Dell International. Their biggest client is Amazon.

In Hinjewadi, Pune, Harish is starting another 1 million sq. ft mixed-use development project, and the group has signed up with PVR Cinemas already. Harish has recently acquired a commercial building, by investing $50 million, in the Magarpatta IT Park, Pune, for which he will collect $5 million in rentals alone.

Mumbai is also finally on Harish's agenda. He has procured land in Prabhadevi, near Worli, in the city. His plans to construct a seventy-storeyed Hilton there were dashed to the ground on account of oversupply of rooms in the city. Now, he has alternative plans for commercial development at the site.

Malls are not in his plans for Mumbai, and that is why Harish instead acquired a 5 per cent stake for Rs 150 crore in the best retail space in the city, the Phoenix Mills, in 2007. He invested in The Mall, Palladium and St Regis hotel. Through a single company, Harish has acquired exposure to retail malls, commercial and residential property.

Harish's success in private equity deals has spoiled him, as he finds the annual returns of 15 per cent from this industry quite low. The investment in Phoenix Mills was made the year before the Lehman Brothers crash in 2008, when the stock markets worldwide were at an all-time high (the Dow being at 14,100). After the crisis, the Dow fell to below 6,600 (dropping almost 60 per cent). At the time, Harish had investments in stock markets in the US, India and Europe. Uncertainty, volatility in the markets, and insecurities and weaknesses in the global economy brought on a few years of struggle. Harish lay low with his investments, and decided that his next investments would again be long-term ones. So he concentrated on the developments he had initiated and kept his nose to the ground. As always, things have a way of recovering slowly, and the markets rose again steadily, 2013 onwards. The pick-up was slow and steady, but the last few years have been very positive.

Harish seems happy with the Modi government. He feels it signals something very strong for India's business houses and economy. The market is actually bullish, and according to Harish, 'We have finally moved from policy paralysis, where so many corporate decisions were hung. But with the Modi government's corrections, we are now recovering, because the PM has brought in a lot of policies that enable good business and we have inched into a business-friendly environment all over again. The government is definitely making it easy for infrastructure investments, getting rid of all hiccups that might cause any further project delays.'

London Investments

When it was quiet in India, Fabiani ventured out again to the EU and identified two properties in London. The cost of development in London is enormous, doubly so on account of currency differences. The gross sale value of these kinds of projects would easily be around a billion dollars. By virtue being in central London, in Mayfair, the projects are among the most expensive in the world. A three- or four-bedroom apartment would cost the equivalent of Rs 200 crore onwards. Harish's property, Mayfair Park Residences, is strategically situated right opposite the Dorchester Hotel and is also managed by it.

His other development, called The Mansion, is situated in Marylebone, right behind Selfridges. Both the developments are doing pretty well, considering the Brexit situation. Harish himself owns an apartment in one of these fabulous buildings, with the flat estimated to be worth £25 million. Harish's idea has always been to get into business that promised growth in the long run. For instance, he has acquired a stake in a new UK bank, Oak North, that is currently growing very aggressively and is planning an IPO in the next few years. He invested in it after 2008, when most European and UK banks were not equipped to extend loans against any business. But Oak North has performed well under a great team that has taken it to another level. It has shown profits of over a million dollars in the last eighteen months.

When people around the world began to find out about Harish's investments, they began to seek him out. In 2012, he was invited to Boston by Massachusetts Institute of Technology to be a part of a panel on entrepreneurship.

In 2013, Harish was in Boston with his younger daughter, who was shortlisting colleges for admission, when he visited Babson College. He fell immediately in love with it. Since his older daughter, Sonali, was already at the University of Southern California, he wanted his second daughter, Simran, to try a different college. When his daughter accepted admission to Babson, he was invited along with a small group of parents to a dinner hosted by Kerry Healey—the president of the college.

When Healey later met him in New York, she offered him trusteeship on the board of Babson College. Harish was delighted. The university board of trustees consists of leaders in business and family enterprises from all over the world—all highly distinguished individuals, accomplished entrepreneurs and heads of corporations.

Healey had this to say about Harish, 'He has great gravitas and is highly respected by his peers. His soft-spoken wisdom is always immensely valued and people look up to him for guidance on complicated managerial issues. He has also been an advocate for student engagements in entrepreneurial activity and was one of the founding supporters of the Babson India Symposium. He was engaged enthusiastically with our many students from India who look up to him as a leader.'

Harish's daughters, aged twenty-four and twenty-one, are smart young women who have educated themselves and chosen simple lives. They have the choice of joining their father's business later. Sonali has graduated from Marshall School at USC (LA) and now works full-time at Teach for India in Mumbai. Simran graduated in May 2017 in entrepreneurship and economics from Babson College.

Philanthropic Pursuits

Harish always wanted to participate in educational initiatives, whether in India or elsewhere. He says the many acres in his land bank will stand in good stead for educational purposes some day. Healthcare is another of his interests, and he has plans to develop hospitals in townships in Chennai and Pune. But knowing fully well that those are long-term projects, he seized the opportunity when he and Chandru Budhrani, who is a wealthy businessman and a philanthropist from Singapore, were asked to be a part of the Fabiani and Budhrani Heart

Institute in 2006, a flagship unit of Sadhu Vaswani Mission's medical complex. It is a comprehensive cardiac care centre. His father was flown down for the inauguration.

Harish says: 'I want to be of use to the society. Yes! One does feel good in doing good business and bringing in x amount of profit, but the pleasure one derives from actually helping the needy is incomparable to any other feeling on earth.' He also feels that Indian culture should be preserved, and to contribute towards this he has promised funds towards the building of a monument in Kutch (100 km from the region's capital, Bhuj) called Jhulelal Tirathdam. PM Modi has said about this project: 'Your dream is now my dream, I want to see a very tall structure which will be visible from a great distance. This will symbolize the far-sightedness of the Sindhis.'

When I quizzed Harish about why he invested more in real estate than in other sectors, he replied: 'What people see and understand is real estate, because it is brick and mortar, but since my other investments are in a portfolio, they are happily unseen.'

His eyes twinkle as he admits that tech companies are still on his priority list: 'I own shares in all the top companies listed in the US, such as Google, Microsoft, Netflix and Amazon, in good size and value.' But his modus operandi for investment appears to have changed. He is still interested in start-ups in the tech space, but now prefers to invest only if they are already a year into their business and have a certain visibility of revenue and profits. He now invests through a partnership with Infosys (a fund called Xfinity), since the company is more hands-on and a leader in the space. They advise him on which companies to invest in. He notes that in 2000, there were probably 100 companies looking for investment, but now in 2017 the number is possibly 10,000, making it all the more important for investors to make careful choices.

Nothing stops a man like Harish. He is always observing, assimilating, calculating and staying abreast of market needs. Even as recently as April 2017, India Land acquired an 18-acre industrial park in Chennai, half constructed and already rented out to a Japanese company.

The solar energy space also interests Harish, since prices in this sector are falling. In Harish's opinion, a solar power plant will soon be on a par with or cheaper than a thermal power plant since the Indian government is promoting green energy. He foresees being able to produce power and sell it at the price at which the government would want to buy it without any premium or subsidy. Today there are certain restrictions by the state and central governments on the quantity of power that anybody can produce and sell. But these restrictions may ease in the future. Harish is already in ownership of one such plant and is in the process of buying more in Tamil Nadu and Andhra Pradesh. By acquiring ready solar plants, he is learning the business as he visits the sites with his engineers.

He is looking to acquire existing plants that have a production capacity of 100 megawatts (which will translate into revenue of more than Rs 100 crore a year). He has already signed a twenty-five-year power purchase agreement with the government—another example of Harish's preference for long-term investments.

Solar power excites him since it is a new area of growth. And technology continues to be a very strong area of interest for him. He says: 'There's no growth as aggressive as in new technology, starting with mobility, the Internet, driverless cars, cloud computing, artificial intelligence and so much more that cannot even be imagined. We are so privileged to be part of this growth, although our generation had to actually adapt to it. We are actually here to experience the transition.'

Over the years, Harish's way of doing business has changed remarkably. Harish still maintains businesses in many parts of the world, including Spain, London, Dubai and Singapore. In the next fifteen to eighteen months, his rental income will exceed $20 million. He has long-term estate investments but also makes sure that cash flows in every month.

He says: 'I buy land and develop it when I think the returns will be substantially interesting, but if I buy already existing projects that offer me reasonable returns, then I settle for that too [even though they don't provide 25 per cent returns immediately, they will do so in the long run]. I still allocate some of my money to these. Both have their good points.' All this will be in addition to all his developed assets bringing him his income. Harish will soon want to list his rental assets in the form of real estate investment trusts, or REITs.

Harish says his daughters can work wherever they fancy, but they are definitely being groomed for their father's empire. Roopa also realizes this.

Roopa talks about how Harish is still ever-willing to learn. He has an analytical mind, is highly intelligent and remains a very good judge of character on account of his acute powers of perception. He loves to read and to gather as much knowledge as he can, and is ever open to picking up knowledge from youngsters about new technologies, apps and trends. Harish also enjoys art and has collected quite a lot, as can be seen from the beautiful paintings that adorn his office walls.

From the appearance of his neat, paperless desk, it seemed as though Harish is a minimalist. His mannerisms were precise, with no exaggerations as he spoke pleasantly in clipped tones. Very much a lone worker, Harish dislikes any kind of distraction. These are all traits of a successful businessman. He prefers being alone during his working hours because he feels focus is of utmost importance. He prefers his administration to be on a different floor altogether. He allows his managers and CEOs to oversee everything while he focuses mainly on investments, ideas and the like. Harish Fabiani is a major delegator, a non-negotiator and an ideator; in a nutshell, he is a man who does the Sindhi community proud.

Lakhi Group—Dilip Kumar Lakhi

The Family Tree

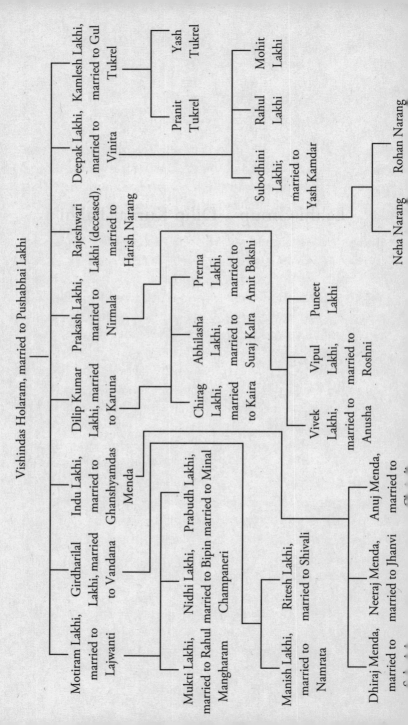

Vishindas Holaram, married to Pushabhai Lakhi

Motiram Lakhi, married to Lajwanti

Girdharilal Lakhi, married to Vandana

Indu Lakhi, married to Ghanshyamdas Menda

Dilip Kumar Lakhi, married to Karuna

Prakash Lakhi, married to Nirmala

Rajeshwari Lakhi (deceased), married to Harish Narang

Deepak Lakhi, married to Vinita

Kamlesh Lakhi, married to Gul Tukrel

Mukti Lakhi, married to Rahul Mangharam

Nidhi Lakhi, married to Bipin Champaneri

Prabudh Lakhi, married to Minal

Manish Lakhi, married to Namrata

Ritesh Lakhi, married to Shivali

Anuj Menda, married to

Dhiraj Menda, married to

Neeraj Menda, married to Jhanvi

Chirag Lakhi, married to Kaira

Abhilasha Lakhi, married to Suraj Kalra

Prerna Lakhi, married to Amit Bakshi

Vivek Lakhi, married to Anusha

Vipul Lakhi, married to Roshni

Puneet Lakhi

Neha Narang

Rohan Narang

Subodhini Lakhi, married to Yash Kamdar

Rahul Lakhi

Mohit Lakhi

Pranit Tukrel

Yash Tukrel

Introduction

Diamonds were discovered in India in the fourth century BC, and except for Borneo, which accounted for a minor supply, India was the world's only source of diamonds until the 1730s. Historically, it was Golconda in India that was known for its diamond mines. Today, the Majhgawan pipe near Panna is India's only diamond source. The hotspots for mining are Australia, Sierra Leone, South Africa and Canada.

Indians were the most prolific diamond polishers in the world, what with their skilled hands and eye for detail. They were also very enterprising. Their secret was that, whether it was in manufacturing, buying or selling, they relied on their strong family support system. This provided them flexibility in operations, and also many willing hands to aid their business. Since they had big family structures, they could afford to have some of their members sent all over the world to expand businesses.

Indian merchants, who are today among the biggest players in the multi-million dollar diamond business, produce 80 per cent of the world's polished diamonds. At least six of the top ten clients of the world's leading diamond company, De Beers, are Indian companies. The lower cost of production in Mumbai, and later in Gujarat, facilitated this. In 2013, India produced 50 per cent, by value, of the polished diamonds the world consumed, and 80 per cent by weight.

The Lakhi Group has a long-standing history in the Indian gem and jewellery industry. It was founded by Dilip Kumar Lakhi's (the current chairman's) grandfather in Shikarpur,

Sindh (now part of Pakistan). The Lakhi family, probably
the only Sindhi family among the big Indian diamond
players, started out very modestly in Jaipur after Partition.
They moved to Mumbai in 1972, where Dilip Kumar Lakhi
established his business in Zaveri Bazaar. They began trading
in precious stones.

The company expanded to manufacture cut and polished
diamonds. The group by now specialized in colourless-
to-brown diamonds in all sizes. The Lakhi Group has also
become one of the largest exporters of diamonds from India
and has perhaps the world's largest diamond polishing factory
in Surat, with over 6,000 workers under one roof.

The chairman of the group, Dilip Kumar Lakhi, is
the driving force behind this mammoth organization. He
came into the media limelight when he became the highest
individual taxpayer in India in 2003, and again when he
bought the famous Cadbury House in Mumbai. Lakhi is a
low-profile individual, but his experience and expertise call
for a deeper look into his life and the history of the Lakhi
Group.

The Lakhis were zamindars settled in Shikarpur. They also had bullion (gold trading) and banking (moneylending) businesses in the pre-Partition days, when most Sindhis were known to be bankers and landlords. Holaram Lekhraj Lakhi was the one who grew the business. Over the years, the family's banking (*kant jo dhando*) network spread from Multan to Kandahar in Afghanistan. The Lakhis belonged to a community now known as the Shikarpuris, who have been moneylenders for many generations. They can be credited with being the inventors of the hundi whereby businessmen and travellers collected money against a small piece of paper that was cleverly used as a financial instrument.

Given that so many families, since their forefathers' times, have changed their last names to suit their circumstances, one wonders if Lakhi was the family's original name. The family's sub-caste (*gotra*) was originally Kalra. In this community, people would change their name to 'Lakhpati' when they earned a lakh of rupees (a princely sum in those days), eventually shortening it to 'Lakhi', which was how the Kalras too acquired this name. They were thought to be lucky for their village, so Lakhi Canal was named after them. Lakhi Canal and Lakhi Gate exist to this day in Shikarpur.

Most of the settlers here were known to be Baniyas and Sahookars. The ones known as Shroffs created the whole network of bankers. They embraced names like Jayutsing, Ram Dass, Dwarka Dass, Chuman Dass, Dula Ram, Lohana, Narayan Dass and Bhatia—all of which had a standing in the field of banking.

It was in Shikarpur itself that the Lakhi family started out in the Indian gem and jewellery industry, the business being set up by Holaram Lakhi. In 1944, the family, then led by Vishindas Holaram Lakhi (Holaram's son), moved to Jaipur. As immigrants, they established their gemstones business here, on the understanding that skilled artisans in the region outnumbered the dealers in the trade. Using very simple wooden handmade tools for their creations, the humble *karigars* (craftsmen) of Jaipur were deemed among the best in India. Like the other families in their community, the Lakhis also started out with the basic Sindhi principle of small margins and high turnover, believing that increasing sales would eventually help expand their profit margins.

First Impression

The iconic Bharat Diamond Bourse in Bandra Kurla Complex in Mumbai is home to Lakhi Group's headquarters, which was where I met the CEO, Dilip Kumar Lakhi.

Dilip was born in May 1950 in Jaipur, which was a jewellery trading centre. He was schooled at the S.S. Jain Subodh Senior Secondary School and went straight into the family business in Delhi after he graduated.

With the reputation of being Mumbai's highest individual taxpayer, topping even other business bigwigs and Bollywood celebrities in the past,[1] Dilip is definitely not your run-of-the-mill billionaire.

The Bharat Diamond Bourse is not an easy place to walk into. The security measures are rigorous, and at any given time the place is teeming with clients and employees. The Lakhi Group moved into the Bourse in 2011. In fact, it was the first company to move in lock, stock and barrel and operate entirely out of there. To date, the industry recognizes that if it wasn't for the Lakhi Group, most of the city jewellers would still be operating out of their same old hub at Opera House in Mumbai. The Lakhis had none other than Varda Shine, managing director of Diamond Trading Company and other colleagues from De Beers inaugurating their office. The group has been a dependable name for its customers and a valued supplier in the trade. Varda recognized these qualities, and for these very same reasons fondly titled the Lakhi Group as the 'diamantaires' diamantaire'. The title has stuck, as the group's core customers are indeed many major diamantaires.

It was a proud moment for this business, which has spanned over six decades and generations of the Lakhi family, to move into its 'new home', as Dilip calls it. The Bourse is truly world class and rivals many of the diamond facilities across the globe. It consists of 2 million sq. ft, with banks, restaurants, Wi-Fi facilities, online trading, pick-up and drop-off facilities, testing laboratories (certified to international standards), diamond equipment and trading halls.

---

[1] Meena Nichani and Dibeyendu Ganguly, 'Diamond Merchant Is Taxmen's Darling', *Economic Times*, 2003, http://economictimes.indiatimes.com/diamond-merchant-is-taxmens-darling/articleshow/45348.cms.

My one-on-one meeting with Dilip Kumar Lakhi was at the group's 6,000 sq. ft office at the Bourse. After his warm handshake, I felt a little more comfortable, though not totally at ease. Even though there were facilities and conveniences around, including elaborate armchairs, Dilip stood throughout our conversation. It was clear he does not dress flamboyantly either. He allows his persona to do all the talking. He is highly moralistic, direct in his ways and heavily rooted in his convictions. He pursues his point to the end. His own chair is very basic, devoid of any unnecessary frills, pretty much like his life, one suspects. He says what he means and means what he says.

Initially, his tone is almost brusque—'I will give you just fifteen minutes and then go for my next meeting.' But his manner eases as he goes on to impress me, this time with his utter simplicity. It is the exact way he does business, with this completely no-nonsense attitude. During demonetization, when people's ire was pouring forth, the country's highest taxpayer in the diamond business was endorsing the move and PM Modi with such fervour that it seemed unreal. He says, 'Whenever a man thinks about tax evasion, he loses focus on his business.'

Few actually know of his projects, since Dilip is not fond of publicity, preferring the cover of anonymity. Dilip is a self-made man who attributes his success to the principles laid down by his father. He says it is only because of his father's blessings, coupled with the support of his four brothers located in different countries, that he has reached his current position.

The Lakhi Group has been a trailblazer. It is one of the largest manufacturers in India. The group supplies to many leading diamond and jewellery businesses and offers more than 5,800 diamond assortments, marketed under its trademark slogan, 'The Power of Choice'. This is the cornerstone of Lakhi Group's services. It is the only company in the world which has branded loose and polished stones, and the only one which doesn't require a jewellery collection to associate with. Their small stones are often referred to as 'certified smalls'. In fact, what GIA (Gemological Institute of America) is for larger stones, Lakhi's goods are for small stones.

The family treats the business as more than just an enterprise, simply because it has had the rich experience of six to seven generations in this business. Their research and development, their integrity and the resoluteness that marks their decisions have brought them to this enviable position.

Foray into the Business

While learning business values and skills from his father, Vishindas Lakhi, Dilip also imbibed his struggle and spirit. Dilip got into the system at the age of fourteen. He would study for a few hours and then work in the family business, a practice that is not uncommon in Sindhi families. Young men end up doing both studies and business in order to learn on the job, and this coaches them as no other institution can.

Dilip attributes the initial success of the company to his father, and calls him an undeniable force in his work life. He blended traditions with modern reality, and reinforced in the family a commitment to excellence—something that survives to this day. Dilip says he has followed his father's transparency, his ethical practices and customer-friendly policies to this day. He says it is the Lakhi Group's consistency in service that has helped it retain a strong position in the global market.

As a teenager, Dilip would make trips to Tiruchirappalli in Tamil Nadu to obtain gemstones, assisting his brother, Girdharilal, who was already managing the business in Delhi. Soon his father changed base to Mumbai, and Dilip, at twenty-two, was put in charge of the storefront in Zaveri Bazaar. At the time he assisted in the business of freshwater pearls. This was a major segment for the family, as the company accounted for at least 90 per cent of the pearls imported from China.

By 1972, the country had emerged as the front runner in the diamond processing industry. Seeing this shift in trend, the Lakhi Group in 1976 forayed into the diamond business. It was Dilip's efforts that took them such a long way ahead. The group today is the market leader in the country and has put India on the global map by building Asia's (with their associates) largest factory, which has housed 6,000 workers under one roof since the early 1990s. The group went on to become the first company in India to produce more than one million carats of polished diamonds per annum. And they retained this position for three consecutive years (1999–2001).

In 1979, the group opened offices in Antwerp, Belgium, which were headed by brothers Prakash and Moti Lakhi. The group was gradually earning its place in a market totally dominated by Gujaratis. It was a time when Dilip's father used to still come in to work every day, assisted by his younger son, Deepak. Their father's advice was well taken by the family, and the group moved on to become the key customer of Hindustan Diamond Company, a subsidiary of De Beers in collaboration with the Government of India, over 1984–1994. The HDC supplied to the local market.

The Lakhi Group's reputation had by now grown by leaps and bounds. Dilip—being the main driving force behind the group's operations—managed the business from Mumbai, along with his brothers, Girdharilal and Deepak. Till today, the immediate family members still hold all the key positions. Dilip's son, Chirag, and Girdharilal's two sons, Ritesh and Manish, gradually joined the business and now help with manufacturing and sales. All three hold positions as vice-presidents today.

By 1991, Dilip's brother-in-law, Gul Tukrel, and sister, Kamlesh, had started their own diamond business in Canada. Dilip's eldest brother, Motilal, who was in Antwerp, had recently moved to Hong Kong. Dilip's younger brother, Prakash, who was initially in Antwerp, moved to New York, while his youngest brother, Deepak, established an office in Dubai, managing the wholesale business and exports. Thus a good network of offices was built across the globe, at all the international hubs for precious metal and stone.

Diamond Trading Company (DTC) in London was their next stop. In 1993, DTC nominated the Lakhi Group as sightholders, according to their norms. The Lakhis had finally won a place with the best through sheer hard work. In the early 2000s, DTC chose the group as one of the top five manufacturers for the Nakshatra Jewellery Programme (that India's premier retail brand Nakshatra had launched for jewellery along with designer clothing). With guidance from his sister, Renu Menda, her husband, Ghanshyamdas Menda, and their sons, Dheeraj, Neeraj and Anuj, Dilip established Studio Reves in 2001. It went on to become India's first-ever designer jewellery studio, after which the group set up a jewellery marketing arm in New York (2002), headed by Dilip's brother, Prakash, and his nephew, Ritesh.

The Lakhis went on to become specialists in the trading of diamonds of all shapes and sizes, from brown to colourless to white. With the tagline 'Diamonds for Everyone Forever', the Lakhi Group sought to make diamonds everyone would aspire to own. This was appreciated by Gary Ralfe, managing director of DTC. The group's activities had now expanded horizontally across the globe, and vertically into the jewellery business. It was now one of the major exporters of diamonds and among the largest producers of small diamonds in the world.

A Man with a Reputation

To know a man's character, the best bet is to talk to his friends. Navratan Sipani of M. Sipani Exports, a Marwari gentleman close to Dilip, gave me quite an insight into the diamond maverick. Having met when they were younger, they had both set their sights big. Already a pearl vendor at the time, Dilip was first introduced to Navratan, who was six years younger, by the latter's uncle in 1979.

Navratan was only just starting out. They struck up a friendship immediately as Dilip was friendly and more than willing to guide and help Navratan. They were both from Rajasthan (Dilip was from Jaipur and Navratan from Bikaner) and bonded over the similarities their families shared.

In the early period of his career, Dilip was in the pearl business, dealing with Japan and China. But with the changing trends and the slump in the wholesale business of pearls, he gradually ventured into the diamond segment. Navratan was Dilip's neighbour when they moved into adjoining offices at Prasad Chambers (in the Opera House area in Mumbai) from Vendaker Mansion and Parekh Market. Having different businesses at the time, they would frequently discuss market trends.

Navratan says Dilip was already known for his high morals and ethics in the diamond market. The group has created a strong identity for itself over the years in the way it dealt with everybody. Buyers had to visit the group's office personally for all transactions. No goods ever left its premises on the basis of an order received by virtual communication.

Prices were always fixed and the group did not encourage haggling, simply because it dealt in the best. Dilip's genius in assortment is also recognized far and wide. The emphasis has always been on customer satisfaction, so much so that if anyone was disappointed with a blind decision, Lakhi always rectified it the next time around, giving the customer absolutely no reason to complain. This helped people develop immense trust in the group and its products.

In terms of metrics, the Lakhi Group is among the top five companies in the trade, their competitors being Rosy Blue India Pvt Ltd, Blue Star, Mahendra Bros Exports Pvt Ltd, Kiran Gems Pvt Ltd and Dimexon International. A notable detail is that Dilip has risen to the top among a concentration of Palanpuri and Kathiawadi diamond merchants—a strong Gujarati bastion.

With his hard work and systems, he has carved a niche for himself. In 1993, the DTC recognized the Lakhi Group, its ways of working and their immense name in the market and chose them as one of the companies from India to sell their rough wares to. It is immensely prestigious to be a sightholder. The DTC chooses eighty-three companies worldwide and fifty-three from India, offering them a three-year contract (which is renewable), and then supplies them a certain amount of rough wares every month for further manufacturing purposes. These sightholders then polish the rough wares, the final products of which are sold to other diamond traders at a premium.

In this business, customers go back to a company solely because of the genuineness of the product it offers and how much they can trust the company. Dilip, standing like Napoleon Bonaparte at the helm of Lakhi Group, has created both in abundant measure. The group doesn't take bank loans, and pays well in advance for all its transactions. But it sells on its own terms. In general, companies in the diamond industry have heavy debts. The Lakhi Group is among the few companies in this field that are debt-free.

I ask Dilip's Marwari friend if Dilip's manner of conducting business is typically Sindhi. Navratan ponders for a good while, then says: 'No offence to the others in the community, but Dilipbhai stands out completely.' Once his mind is made up, there's no going back. He chooses whom he sells to and he decides how he wants to sell. Navratan feels both the Sindhi and Marwari communities have a unique similarity in their working patterns—tight-fistedness, but with an ability to earn. Dilip has changed his working style to suit the market he works in, adapting his Sindhi ways to Jain business tactics.

Dilip's friend and broker, Anand Mehta of Prankit Exports, first met him ten years ago and remembers Dilip from his Parekh Market days. Today, Prankit Exports still does business with the Lakhi Group. Anand says Dilip's way of working is quite unique as he only makes cash purchases because they are cheaper, but when he sells, he gives the customer time to make his payment, in the interim collecting a minimal interest on the same transaction. Being cash-rich, the banks support him wholeheartedly, and this goodwill results in tremendous business. Strangely, adds Anand, it has always worked out that no matter at what price one buys from Dilip, when the goods go on to be sold, one invariably gets to make a profit.

The Lakhi Group has spent four decades mastering the manufacture and sorting of diamonds, and the result is the extraordinary range of precise assortments. People recognize their diamonds, which they refer to as 'Lakhi assortment' or 'Lakhi goods'. The secret is that Dilip has trained his staff rigorously, and is aware of the unique global reputation his assortment system has. Dilip says polished loose diamonds are always the essential component of any finished piece of diamond jewellery and that he is always open to changing the parameters to make palpable improvements.

He agrees that his father was the actual pioneer of the business, teaching him that the only way to progress was continuous self-improvement. Every day, he says, he consciously adopts a willing, open and ready-to-learn attitude when he enters his workplace. And when he leaves work in the evening, he feels like a graduate. He says, 'I don't think I am ever going to feel like a complete person. I am always searching, ever evolving.'

People tend to credit Dilip with many positive attributes, often because they have come to expect them in a man of his reputation and stature. He sighs, and says, 'People have put a lot of faith in me, and sometimes it gets difficult for me to live up to it. In the film *Guide*, I remember people repeatedly prodding Dev Anand, ultimately turning him into a *sadhu*. Similarly, in the diamond market, being called a charitable man pushes me to play the part.' For example, when people such as Arun Kumar of Rosy Blue describe him as the Yudhishthira of the diamond market, it tends to pressure Dilip to be more magnanimous than he already is.

The group has nearly forty years of experience in developing close relationships with customers, not just supplying them with diamonds but also advising them on business and marketing strategies, integrating their systems and processes, gaining their trust and acting as a dependable anchor when the markets are volatile. People lap up Dilip's advice on current developments and business. They throng to his offices to buy from him, to chat with him, or to catch a meal with him if they can. Dilip has also never been known to sidestep any person or company that one of his friends or associates has introduced him to. Tongue in cheek, Anand says this is something a Gujarati businessman would never do. However, Dilip is ethical in every way.

When demonetization took place, Dilip benefited from it because market sentiment weakened and the cost of roughs (smaller sizes) dropped drastically while the sales of his polished soared—truly a win-win situation for him.

Russell Mehta, heir to Rosy Blue and managing director of one of the largest diamond houses in Mumbai, is a contemporary of Dilip Lakhi's. His luxurious office, also located in the Bharat Diamond Bourse, overlooks the rest of the complex. He seems so comfortable talking about Dilip that one would imagine that they are best friends. In reality, they have worked well together and have respect based on affection for each other.

Initial meetings are always special, and they usually determine what the person will mean to you after that. Russell clearly remembers his first brush with Dilip. Rosy Blue, a sightholder with DTC, has been in the business for close to sixty years. The Lakhi Group is a younger company; Russell himself came into the business in the late 1980s. In the beginning, DTC chose its sightholders based on factors such as the company's standing, turnover, capital and capabilities, but the deciding criteria were unclear. Getting an association with DTC was like a scholar getting chosen to go to Princeton or Harvard.

As a sightholder, Russell was tasked with fulfilling some clients' orders, and he was looking for a certain quality of diamonds. At the time, Dilip worked out of Parekh Market, but the places that emerged as jewellery hubs were Prasad Chambers and Pancharatna building. It was here that Russell happened to come across a packet of gorgeous black-spotted naats (colourless diamonds with dark inclusions), which belonged to a certain Dilip Lakhi.

Intrigued, he quizzed the broker, got introduced to the supplier and completed his purchase. Russell was duly impressed, because knowing the nature of the diamond market and, most importantly, knowing how haggling eventually sealed a deal, it was very refreshing for him to work with Lakhi, who never resorted to bargaining. They did a fair amount of business in the years that followed, since Lakhi was good at sharing business forecasts and stepped up his polishing just for Russell.

Dilip always made for a very unique business partner; he set his own rules and game plan while still staying ethical and principled. Most people work with the mindset of raking in the bucks, seizing all the opportunities they can, but Dilip stands out on that score, as he has made his life more about moral values rather than money. Nothing has changed about Dilip in the last twenty years, comments Russell. His personality and character have remained the same even though Lakhi Group has now grown a hundred fold and is among the top five in the Indian diamond market.

Today, one can perhaps only hear whispers in the diamond market of the numbers associated with the business families in the industry, since they all keep their secrets close to their chest. Things have definitely changed in the diamond merchant community since its move into the big offices in Bharat Diamond Bourse. Now, one's fortunes dictate one's standing. Earlier, there was a robust camaraderie among the businessmen, as they visited each other's offices without seeking formal appointments; attended marriages and funerals in the community and even holidayed together as families. The dictates of the new business culture have made them more formal and corporate.

'A man to reckon with', 'a stalwart of sorts', 'a man of uniqueness' . . . is how Dilip is described in the market. And this is the very reason he was allowed entry into such a Gujarati-dominated profession. He easily fitted in and has held his own ever since. Russell laughs out loud at the saying:

'If you see a Sindhi and a snake, avoid the Sindhi.' He says Dilip has never belonged in this category. In business, most people go to him for help and guidance. He has contributed towards changing the reputation the Sindhi community had unfortunately gained.

'My word is my bond' is the maxim that most people in the diamond industry go by. And this is more than true for Dilip. At one time, Russell's son, Viraj, who had joined the diamond business, was concluding some deal with Dilip that Russell was completely unaware of. The prices were fixed and everything was finalized. Dilip then called Russell and told him how much he loved Viraj and his thought process; and just to make sure that he stayed on in the diamond business, he was going to further offer him a 1 per cent reduction on the deal in spite of having sealed it. Russell was totally blown away. 'I have been in the business for thirty-three years and never heard of anybody giving a discount after a deal is concluded.' Clearly, Dilip likes to create trust and help people at any cost, and is keen that the younger generation takes over.

I ask Russell if it is true that Dilip buys in cash and sells under certain terms, allowing the buyer to take a fixed amount of time to pay up and charging a fee on the delayed payment. Russell confirms that the Lakhi Group is extremely cash-rich. It is well-known that in the diamond industry, most merchants borrow from banks for their working capital. But Dilip does not do so. Russell is also impressed with Dilip's philanthropic style, though he feels a lot of money is directed towards religious purposes and more can be donated for education because that is where the country's future lies.

Diamond companies, unlike other corporations, do not actively participate in CSR, but end up giving more than anybody else. In the diamond trade, far more than people can ever imagine goes out in the name of charity. For example, jewellers support many religious activities (a large number of them being Gujarati Jains) and donate prolifically to educational institutions. Most of them, however, never speak about their charitable activities.

Biju Patnaik, executive vice-president and head of the gems and jewellery segment at IndusInd Bank, Mumbai, has been doing business with the Lakhis since 1997. Dilip had been banking with ABN AMRO all along till part of this business of the bank was sold to IndusInd in 2015. Predictably, Dilip moved with the business.

Patnaik agrees that in the midst of the three noteworthy business communities in India (the Gujaratis, Marwaris and Sindhis) Dilip stands out. Dilip is unlike other traders in the sense that he is known for his straight talk and is always extremely particular about paying tax. Dilip is known to pay proportionately higher income tax than many of his peers, his explanation being that the country needs the money for infrastructure to run schools and colleges, and people have to step up to do the needful.

Dilip is loyal towards everything he holds dear, and Patnaik remembers his words with affection—'You are my bank and you will be my only bank'. Patnaik feels that Dilip, at his level of business at the time of moving to IndusInd, was taking more risk with joining the bank than the bank was with him, since he is well-known the world over for never borrowing money to do any kind of transaction. How does that happen with Dilip, when businessmen always part borrow while putting their own money into their business? Some of the reasons could be that his capital is very much kept within the country and that he knows how to invest his money to get better returns than what banks could ever offer him by way of interest. Being a very astute businessman, he has ways of choosing the right investments, be it in the diamond business, in shares (long-term investments) or in companies themselves.

Patnaik also shares an instance of Dilip's generosity to a school in Jaipur. Dilip helped ABN AMRO on a project conducted by an NGO called Support, which involved the rehabilitation of street children, weaning them off harmful addictions and looking after them for fifteen years. They were then helped to gain an education or were provided vocational guidance so they could eventually stand on their own feet. Dilip funded the entire lot's requirement of medicines for their detox treatment for fifteen years.

Though known to be on everybody's friends' list, Dilip himself does not subscribe to having too many friends. He is choosy in picking his close buddies. He's more of a family man, and people around him feel that his son, Chirag, is very much following in his father's footsteps, just as Dilip had in his father's. Over their twenty-year relationship, Biju Patnaik says he has never seen Dilip misbehave with or insult people, or even take anyone to task. Dilip has a very interesting way of managing all his interpersonal relationships. He expects good work and hires only the best. If any employee causes him distress, he complains about him but insists he should not be fired.

As Patnaik seems to know Dilip so closely, I ask him why a man of this stature is not listed in *Forbes*. He laughs and says this is because Dilip does not need his wealth to be measured. His personal wealth itself is believed to be close to a billion dollars or more. 'A man wealthier in heart than in possessions,' is how Patnaik describes him.

Ashok Hinduja, chairman of the Hinduja Group of companies (India), also knows Dilip intimately, not only as a friend but also as his relative. Being of the same age, they grew up sharing the love and affection of Ashok's mother, who was a very benevolent soul. She treated Dilip's mother as her own daughter, since Dilip's grandmother was her older sister. Ashok has very fond memories of his cousin. He remembers how his large-hearted mother gave gifts to everybody who walked into her bungalow in Khar. One particular incident stands out for Ashok when Dilip was the happy recipient of something that was Ashok's favourite item; this did not go down well with Ashok. However, she convinced her son that things could always be replaced but people could not and had to be treated well.

She would take Dilip along to all the charitable institutions and hospitals she visited. Dilip recalls that seeing his *masi* share her life and belongings selflessly with so many is what first inspired him. Ashok says his father always believed that donating money is one thing but the effort of going to somebody's home or office and raising money is the more difficult activity.

Ashok remembers one visit to Dilip's office, when he took along the chief of the Kharghar ISKCON Temple, where he chairs the development of the hospital. They requested a donation from Dilip for the project. Dilip silently cut him a cheque of Rs 25 lakh immediately. Ashok's face softens as he speaks about his cousin, calling him humble, down-to-earth and a very practical person who never refuses to help a good cause.

Ashok talks of his cousin's simplicity and how Dilip has remained his intrinsic self, often refusing to get a better car or a bigger house, and even maintaining the same ethics in business as he always did. It is far more important for Dilip to grow his business than to be materialistic, observes Ashok.

Ashok adds that Dilip is one of those who honours his word, whether he loses or makes money on account of it. Because of his integrity, simple lifestyle and endearing personality, Ashok has his cousin on the board of the governing council of the Hinduja Hospital and as a trustee in the Hardwar Chatandev Kutty Ashram.

Dilip learnt at the feet of his father, as the obedient son who got his knack for business from just watching the previous generation at work. Understandably now, he has fine-tuned the business according to the times. Ashok admires the way he has structured the business to accommodate his joint family, taking into account all the brothers and their families, despite the fact that they all now live separately and tend to different parts of the business all over the world.

The promoters of another DTC sightholder, Mahendra Brothers, also had a word to say about their long-term association with Dilip. The Pancharatna building has been the landmark and address of many a jeweller of repute in India over the years. Jitu Kaka, head of Mahendra Group, is an old admirer of Dilip. He says Dilip has the reputation he does today because he treats even the smallest buyer with respect.

He talks about how Dilip has helped even those buyers who were short of money, giving them payment windows with time frames that entailed only minimal interest. Living a life of partial retirement now, Jitu Kaka and his family still like dealing with Dilip and his family.

Clearly, Dilip is held in high esteem by close associates, business partners and even competitors. It is known in the industry that he was always been consistent in his wares since he has had a monopoly over brown diamonds and the smaller ones. His simple and clean-cut way of dealing with people has consistently attracted loyal customers and associates.

Being Ahead of the Game

Taking care of the customer has always been the mantra at Lakhi Group. The transparency of their transactions, coupled with their fixed and fair prices, creates a space where customers are offered an optimum buying experience. The reason people buy from them is because of the high quality of diamonds they sell. They are also known to employ the best craftsmen and technology.

Most of the orders at Lakhi Group are received over the phone and by email from wholesalers and top manufacturers across the world. But they have to be picked up personally.

At the group, quality is key, and the company is considered a barometer for the market. Dilip encourages his people to use all the knowledge and expertise they have gathered over the years in manufacturing diamonds to improve design and development. Their consistent quality, coupled with reliable supply, has created very loyal customers. Eighty-five per cent of Lakhi's turnover is from repeat orders. All of this adds value to the group's brand equity.

Known to share his know-how with the entire diamond industry, Dilip also cooperates with other agencies to facilitate newer and better methods of manufacturing diamonds, along the way safeguarding the interests of the industry by making sure all the rules are followed. He has also been known to settle quarrels, arbitrating in disputes within the community and saving people the bother of recourse to the courts.

The managers at Lakhi Group are asked to follow a strict discipline, and the workers encouraged to do their best. Dilip pays attention to the minutest details at his facilities, this being ensured by quality evaluation by experts from time to time. Part of the group's success is also due to its eagerness to embrace new technology and research and development. Technical experts and buyers from the developed countries are invited to visit their factories to provide inputs and help them grow further.

With a strong emphasis on hiring the right people, Dilip looks for three characteristics in an employee—efficiency, loyalty and responsibility. He also strongly believes in grooming and promoting people. He makes sure that even the less educated among his employees are given ample opportunities to rise if they try hard enough; they become successful managers, and sometimes entrepreneurs.

The Lakhi Group has an excellent support system in its numerous stakeholders, members of the immediate family who form the board, employees and technology partners. Dilip has strategically hinged his business on labour and management and not purely on production, quality and technology. He chooses executives who are not driven by the pay packet alone, simply because he believes that his workers are his partners in profit, deserving the same respect and right to a decent living, and refers to them as co-workers and co-owners.

Strangely, despite the group's high turnover, its marketing costs have always been zero. About his strategy, Dilip says he used to travel overseas seven times a year, from 1978 till 2010 (to America, Europe, China, etc.), but they were all buying trips, never to actually sell his wares or for PR or marketing. The group's main aim has been to produce diamonds of every quality for everyone. Its factories produce polished goods worth $100 to $100,000, side by side.

Mumbai has been the group's main office and hub for the longest time, while Surat is where its factories are located. The group employs more than 7,000 people. Lakhi takes special care of their well-being but does not claim to do anything for effect. He clearly says the only things of utmost importance to him are god, his intellect and his client, in that order. His way of working, by his own admission, is different from that of the average businessman. He stays in the system but works according to his own methods.

Philanthropic Pursuits

Business is clearly Lakhi's profession, but public service is his passion. A believer in humanitarian causes, Dilip says he does not believe in caste, colour or creed. But he does have RSS leanings, following in the footsteps of his forefathers. For public welfare activities, he has drawn up a clear list of areas that his companies, business and enterprises are to be associated with. The list includes education, healthcare, vocational training, cultural promotion, upkeep of religious heritage, provision of shelters and village uplift. All these welfare activities have been overseen by the Lakhi Trust since 1987.

Dilip is known to move his money around very well, earning it and investing it long-term, but he says, quite modestly, 'First and foremost, all this money belongs to god, I am merely the custodian. Even my body is not mine. That's the reason I don't call the money I give away "charity or donation". I call it my contribution.' Money for good causes is never given in the name of one person; the Lakhi Family is always the contributor.

For the Lakhi Group, the entire concept of social responsibility is linked with building hospitals, schools and educational institutions. Some of the beneficiaries of the Lakhi Trust are St Mira Brotherhood School, Friends of Tribals Society, hospitals like Bhagwan Mahaveer Cancer Hospital (Jaipur), Girivihar Hospital, Kesharchand Foundation Trust and Medical Research Foundation, Mahajan Hospital at Palanpur, Mavjat Hospital, and a hospital in Saurashtra. Contributions have also gone out to Indian Institute of Gems & Jewellery National Relief Foundation, Bhavnath Chanalal Arogyayanidhi, and towards the construction of houses for victims of the tsunami of 2004, the Gujarat earthquake of 2001 and floods in many places in the country.

In the matter of religion, Dilip has been more than generous, since he has always been of the opinion that one has to preserve the Hindu religion. He has donated a gold throne, an entrance gate made of real gold and gold statues, collectively weighing more than 180 kg, to the famous shrines of Badrinath, Somnath and Dwarka, to the Jain Temple at Mahudi, and to the statue of Bhagwan Mahavir, Pavapuri. The Somnath temple in Gujarat has also been the recipient of 109 kg of gold. Creating an influx of devotees to the temple, this donation has improved the livelihood of the people living around the shrine.

Industrialist Sarita Mansingka of Tania Industries, (soybean and edible oil manufacturers) discovered a brother in Dilip when she came into contact with him fifteen years ago. Sarita and her husband run an NGO, Friends of Tribals Society (Ekal Vidyala Foundation). They had heard about Dilip's contributions to society, and met him through a common friend. Dilip was visibly impressed with their work, but he noticed that Sarita's husband had a habit of chewing paan masala. He remarked that if her husband wanted any help from the Lakhi Group, he would have to make choice and give up the bad habit. Dilip said he was ready to invest in a person who would take the project a long way and not somebody who had no regard for his own life. That right decision on Sarita's husband's part got him Rs 29 lakh fifteen years ago.

Sarita then organized for Dilip a 'van yatra' into the tribal areas. Dilip was moved and agreed to contribute 1 per cent of the cost of all 55,000 schools under the project, which would amount to more than Rs 1 crore annually. Today he is easily one of their largest contributors, though he does not like to publicize this fact.

Friends of Tribals Society has already adopted close to 55,000 schools in small villages, 2,000 of them on behalf of Dilip. Their primary job is to educate children. The education can happen in a hut, in a temple or simply under a tree, employing exactly one teacher from the village itself. Children are educated up till class three. Students who show an inclination to continue their education are helped with admission to government schools. This costs the foundation Rs 20,000 per year. The children are not given uniforms or offered free food, the idea being to teach them how to stand on their own feet. The NGO has thirty-three chapters all over India, helping tribal people living under the poverty line in the country (currently 8 crore). Sarita has worked for twenty-five years on this project. Her dream is to set up 1 lakh schools.

Dilip's contributions to the education sector include a new wing for S.V. Public School in Jaipur, a city close to his heart. The group also donated to a school in Mehsana, where the complex was named after Dilip's father, called Shri Vishindas Holaram Vidya Sankul.

There are several projects supported anonymously by Dilip, because he is not interested in garnering name or fame for them. When there are national calamities, the group always chips in. It stepped in to help with donations for the Orissa cyclone, the Gujarat earthquake and the Kargil War.

Awards

In 2009, the managing director of DTC, Varda Shine, presented the JJS Gold Souk Award to Dilip Lakhi for his outstanding contributions to the gems and jewellery industry. He has also been recognized by the Sindhi community, and received the Outstanding Citizen Award by the Sindhi

Chamber of Commerce in 2001. He was awarded the Jaipur Shree 2013 by Jaipur Pravasi Sangh—an association that awards prominent personalities who have their roots in Jaipur. Then came the Lifetime Achievement Award by the Gems and Jewellery Export Promotion Council in 2014–2015. In March 2016, Dilip Lakhi was given the Lifetime Achievement Award at the India Gems and Jewellery Awards ceremony in Jaipur.

A Keen Investor

Dilip also deals in equity, being a large investor in the sharemarket. He figures on the top ten list of equity investors in India. A long-term investor, Dilip has stakes in many companies in other sectors he feels bullish on, and continues to invest wisely. He has always known how to make money faster than most others. None of his banks and wealth managers have met his standards of understanding or implementing his methods. Kalpen Parekh of DSP BlackRock Investment Managers Pvt Ltd, who was once a manager at IDFC, remembers his first meeting with Dilip Lakhi ten years ago, when he was with ICICI Prudential Mutual Fund. Kalpen's job has always been asset management. The first impression he took away from the meeting was that Dilip was a very keen investor with an integrity that was rare.

When Kalpen went to advise him on where to invest and how, he found himself thinking that Dilip could probably teach him a thing or two. Kalpen realized that Dilip, despite his stature, was open to sharing his views, to talk about his early days in Pakistan and how traditional banking was done in a certain way, showing that he understood money while taking the risks required. The emphasis was on the traditional way of banking, wherein risk could be controlled and money was made the legitimate way. What Dilip learned was that in giving people the money they needed and by taking care of one's liquidity, one could still protect one's capital. That reflected Dilip's temperament, and therein lay his guideline for dealing with money throughout his career.

Recognizing Dilip's approach to money, Kalpen was able to advise him accordingly, keeping in mind the fact that Dilip knew more than he did. Both understood that mutual funds have the big advantage of giving returns that are tax-efficient. That he could liquidate them at a short notice also suited Dilip. Being a brilliant investor, Dilip today manages his own stocks. But fixed income and bonds are not that tax-friendly when bought on one's own, so he needed the advising company for that.

In his conversations with Dilip, Kalpen keeps his contribution minimum because he wants to learn more from Dilip—his analysis of business opportunities, his evaluation of risk and his understanding of business at the ground level. Dilip has a great understanding of all this because he follows the headlines, realizes how cycles contribute to the movement of money, and how employment works in smaller companies—basically, he knows how to join all the dots before investing.

Kalpen observes that many big businesses survive by cutting costs, and use practices that might be frowned upon. Sometimes they try to hurt the competition. But the Lakhi Group is different. It has created an empire on its own terms.

Keeping Traditions Alive

The Lakhi Group is a family-run business. Today Dilip is the face of the company, which was painstakingly built by his father, Vishindas Holaram Lakhi, along with his five sons, Motiram, Girdharilal, Dilip, Prakash and Deepak. They function as a joint family that resides in different parts of the world. The sons of the five brothers are all in the business, spearheading different departments. Dilip handles the Mumbai operations along with his son Chirag, his brother, Girdharilal, and his two sons Manish and Ritesh. The brothers, Motiram, Prakash and Deepak, head operations in Hong Kong, New York and Dubai, respectively. The Lakhis are strict vegetarians and teetotallers.

A small-town boy, Dilip grew up loving all games, from kite-flying to kho kho, volleyball and cricket, just as most young boys would. His schooling was derailed for a while because his school didn't have extra seats for children who didn't know Hindi. Since he had free time, he would travel 4 km every day to work in his father's office. He also caught up with the level of Hindi that was required in school. However, he was a little unhappy with the situation of having to work, since he was just a child. In retrospect he feels it was the right thing to do and has no regrets about it.

Married to Karuna Munjal in 1976, Dilip has three children. Reticent and soft-spoken, Karuna has kept the family together and fuelled all of Dilip's charitable causes. Dilip's son, Chirag, was educated in Mumbai, and joined the family business. His daughters, Abhilasha and Prerna, are now married. Prerna, his youngest daughter, lives in Silicon Valley where she has her own start-up. She has always been in awe of her father, and keeps him on a pedestal even today. The utter simplicity of the way they were brought up is her fondest memory of life in her parents' home.

None of the brouhaha of wealth ever touched them, even after they became aware of their father's stature. Educated well, with two postgraduate degrees, one from Harvard and the other from CASS business school, Prerna grew up wanting to be independent and caring but at the same time upholding all the family values. Prerna had an arranged marriage to a self-made Marwari Jain, Amit Bakshi, who is also from an entrepreneurial family.

Both daughters were always treated the same way as their brother and were given the freedom to create their own identities. Prerna would work at the group during her holidays, helping in the marketing and sorting. She even stepped in as a jewellery designer, creating her own clientele. Later she did a course at GIA in New York, furthering her knowledge of the trade. Dilip wanted her to become another Indira Nooyi, as he had set her up for success, grooming her to be conscientious, hardworking and ambitious. He gave her freedom and did not interfere in her activities any way. She learnt that simply listening to him speak showed her the way to success. Dilip has indeed changed with the times, but his one stance has remained the same—his insistence on honesty, on not living on credit, and on not worrying about money as it naturally follows hard work.

Abhilasha, a trained jewellery connoisseur, is married to Suraj Kalra, also a diamantaire, and has two children,

Naman and Nanndika. She lives in a joint family. She is successful at her work and is sought after for her jewellery designs. Chirag is Dilip's only son and is married to Kaira with one son, Dev. They live comfortably in the joint family fold. Strong in his convictions, Chirag has a pretty clear vision of what he wants and how his ideas will work. He has been instrumental in expanding the business across many major countries. Together with his cousins, Manish and Ritesh, he has managed to bring the company up to global standards, while also understanding contemporary art and manufacture of Indian jewellery. They are definitely carrying forward the Lakhi Group's vision and its values and customs. Respect is paramount in this Sindhi family, and it shows in the way the younger generation conducts itself.

In 2013, the media went into overdrive when it received news of Dilip Lakhi buying Cadbury House, a popular south Mumbai landmark, for around Rs 350 crore. Beating realty developers like the Lodha Group, Oberoi Realty and Peninsula Land to the acquisition, Dilip said he was not buying to redevelop it but for personal use. The property was acquired by Cadbury in 1981 and refurbished in 2001. It is an art deco building that sits on 1.1 acres of land on Peddar Road in south Mumbai, just opposite Mahalaxmi temple. It has two structures, a two-storeyed office and an eight-storeyed residential block. The media went berserk trying to know more about the man who had bought such an expensive property, but Dilip shrugged off all the attention. 'I don't know what all this fuss is about, I don't believe I have done anything great,' he said.

The Lakhi Group Today

The Lakhi Group has been among the top companies, calling the shots in the Indian diamond industry, and Dilip has made the rules quite evident. Known for its fixed rates, upfront cash payment for goods and its reputation of being the only debt-free company in the diamond industry, it has created its own identity.

Dilip has always been one to show his strength in difficult markets. He likes to surf against the wind. The group has demonstrated strength and resilience during every crisis. During the 2008–09 crisis, while others were losing their faith in diamonds, the Lakhi Group showed its leadership by continuing to buy roughs in the softening market, thereby supporting the market. It not only increased its workforce by 30 per cent (thus creating more jobs) but its turnover too increased, by 25 per cent. Dilip is of the view that whatever he needs to achieve, he does so in multiples. To be totally satisfied and to be highly successful are two completely different things. Dilip will always be that person who needs to do more. Of course, there have been some failures and disappointments, such as instances of ingratitude on the part of people close to him, but he has learnt all his lessons well. He has been a fighter, always bouncing back even stronger.

He has never really seen dark days, as he has never desired more than what was necessary for his day-to-day living. Dilip fondly remembers a simpler time when he used to feed the birds at Chowpatty Beach (when he could probably afford very little). To date, he is known in some quarters as the gentleman who shops truckloads of stuff every Sunday and distributes it among the needy. He surely doesn't want people to remember him only for his wealth but also for his contribution to life and to the world on a larger scale. He believes that he is merely returning all the debts he was born with.

It is not easy to find in times like this a man whom everyone, from bankers to friends and contemporaries, look up to, as is evident from their testimonials.

Embassy Group—Jitu Virwani

The Family Tree

Motiram Virwani, married to Raj Harjani

Sonu Virwani, married to Sanjeev Wahi
- Sanchita

Jaikishen Virwani, Jaya Hirani (divorced)
- Siddhanth
- Jahnvi

Vandana Sood (divorced) | Jitendra Virwani | Lina Smaltz (married)
- Karan
- Aditya
- Neel
- Natalie

Introduction

The past three decades have seen considerable growth and change in the Indian real estate sector, making India one of the fastest-growing markets in the world. This has attracted both national and international investors. The rapid expansion in the country's population, the substantially higher income levels and exposure among its people has led to a boom in infrastructure. The increased demand for both commercial and residential real estate has had a huge multiplier effect on the economic growth of the country.

Eyebrows went up when the Embassy Group, in partnership with PE player Blackstone, announced in 2014 its acquisition of a 106-acre business park on Outer Ring Road in Bengaluru, simply because it was one of the largest commercial real estate deals in India, worth Rs 2,050 crore. With this purchase, the group had edged out DLF, the country's other commercial office realtor. This deal took the company's total holdings in India to 30 million sq. ft, against DLF's 27.50 million sq. ft.

Jitendra Virwani or Jitu, chairman and managing director of Embassy Group, was ranked No. 68 on *Forbes India*'s 2015 list of the richest, with his personal worth at $1.6 billion. Jitu has by now ably carved a niche for himself in real estate and building, and that has made him a billionaire, not only in the residential and technological spaces, but will soon make him one in the world of industrial parks, logistics and warehouses too.

Some call Jitendra's success story a textbook case study, as he built his business step by step, with intricate planning and strategy. Having started in the real estate business in the 1980s as a small developer, he has been responsible for the Embassy Group's meteoric rise, becoming a kingpin in the business with aplomb. In the last two decades, he has succeeded in building the largest stock of luxury buildings in the office space. The group has also acquired a residential portfolio that caters to a premier clientele.

The Embassy Group has made a permanent mark on India's real estate horizon. It has 1,700 acres of land in India and 37 million sq. ft of prime commercial, residential, retail, hospitality, industrial and warehousing space overseas. As one of the top three real estate brands in India—also named one of 'India's best companies to work for' by *Forbes* in 2015— the group has earned its place in the business of redefining spaces.

Just fifty, Jitendra Virwani or Jitu, as he is fondly known, is found on most days at his Embassy International Riding School, riding, hitting a volley of tennis balls or working out with his personal trainer in the gymnasium. He enjoys living far away from Bengaluru, away from the pollution and chaos of city life. He lives with his wife, Lina, in his beautiful home, Lubimaya (Russian for beloved). This is where he meets me as we discuss his business and philosophy. He sits atop his beautiful horse, Bailey, and surveys his home adjoining the riding school, which houses not just his horses but also his office.

As we sit down to breakfast by the beautiful poolside, he recalls how he never thought this part of his dream would come true, where he could bask in the joy of solitude and huge spaces under the wide open sky.

Humble Beginnings

Born and brought up in Mumbai, Jitu attended Don Bosco High School in Matunga. At school, he excelled in sports, cricket being his main passion. He was considerably influenced by the memory of his mother asking his uncle for money to run their home in times of financial stress. At that early age he decided he would never be helpless or live in fear of an unknown destiny.

His father, Mohandas, was in the business of blasting rocks to lay foundations for buildings. He was the one who laid the foundation stone for the famous Usha Kiran building on Altamount Road in Mumbai. He then went on to make Raj Niketan, a building named after his wife.

Growing up, Jitu saw some members of the Virwani family getting more and more involved in horse racing and gambling. He began to strongly oppose both activities, in principle. The rebel in him emerged, but did not leave any bitterness in him. On the contrary, he felt encouraged to persevere, work hard and prosper so he could get his family out of the dark times. This was when the desire to make money took deep root in him, and he decided to choose a career that would make him financially independent.

Adolescence and Marriage

When Jitu was thirteen, the family moved from Bombay to Bangalore (now Bengaluru). Mohandas wanted to start a new life and expand his business, even if it was in a new city. So he took on a partner and started work on a real estate project called Gulbahar with his brother. Mohandas spent a lot of his time working hard at the site to create a new life for himself and his family. He built his first building, Embassy Centre, on his own. Then followed Embassy Court and Embassy Palace, where he currently resides. His USP was large spaces, which sold with great difficulty at the time (for Rs 14 lakh) but now cost more than Rs 4–6 crore.

Jitu attended Stracy Memorial High School and then Christ College, where he would often bunk classes. He would often go to his father's office, occasionally visiting the construction sites, much to his father's chagrin, because Mohandas wanted his son to concentrate on his college education.

As with all boys of that age, pocket money was always a source of worry. But this Sindhi boy had it in his genes to strive to make ends meet even at that age. At the time, as a result of the Gulf war, the streets of Bengaluru were teeming with Iraqi and Iranian students, selling their possessions and other wares for some extra pocket money. Jitu started a regular trade, buying pistachios from them and selling at Sindhi General Stores on Commercial Street, as there was high demand for pistachios, especially from elderly Sindhi women. Buying at Rs 65 a kg, he would sell the nuts at Rs 100 a kg to the storekeeper, who would in turn sell them for Rs 180 a kg.

Thus a bargain was struck, and Jitu became a young entrepreneur. Slowly he did away with the middleman too and started selling directly to his mother's kitty group, giving them the middleman's discount. This kept his pockets full. At eighteen, his life was filled with snooker and pistachios. Partying became an integral part of his existence, since he was always flush with cash and did not have to beg or borrow. His father helped him get his first car, a second-hand Mark 4 Ambassador in his first year of BCom, when not many boys owned any means of transport of their own.

But Mohandas knew exactly when to pull the reins. He put Jitu, then nineteen, in charge of the Embassy Palace project. This property on Cunningham Road was awaiting government approval. Jitu was definitely cut out for the job, as he loved getting his hands dirty, chatting with the Gujarati contractors and simultaneously learning the ropes of the business. He got his adrenalin rush filling the gaps between the slabs with newspapers, counting the cement bags that came in, buying sand etc. And in the evenings he would party hard. He felt he had the best of both worlds.

At around the same time, Jitu met his first wife, Vandana, in college. They went on to get married and have three children. He married Vandana in 1989, when he was just twenty-two, being very impressed with her traditional values. But later he found her immensely headstrong.

Karan, their first-born, came into the world two and a half years after their marriage. His birth changed their lives, as firstborns usually do, filling their lives with joy. Work was prospering and the family moved into Embassy Palace, Jitu's very first project, which was built under his father's supervision. Aditya was born two-and-a-half years later, but by then the marriage had deteriorated considerably. Trust issues reared their ugly head. Even in this period of unrest, they had a third son, Neel, who is today the apple of Jitu's eye. But nothing could save the marriage, and Jitu and Vandana split after eighteen years of marriage.

In the interim, Jitu's sister, Sonu, married Sanjeev Sood and moved to Delhi, but later shifted back to Bengaluru to join the family business. So did Jitu's brother, Jaikishen.

Prolific Dealmaker

Life continued to take its course as Jitu's father, who had actually started life afresh at forty-six, looked for a new working partner to share his responsibilities with. Business was growing at a rapid pace, but Mohandas's brother and his children did not want to continue living in Bengaluru. So they parted ways in 1983, and Mohandas joined hands with a new partner, Sarogi. In the fallout with his brother, Mohandas had taken one property, the Ambassador Hotel, for himself, but changed its name to Embassy Centre, which gave the group its name. As 50–50 partners, Mohandas and Sarogi formed a good team, with Mohandas executing the work and Sarogi managing the finances.

By now Jitu had become pretty ferocious in the business, taking some important decisions by himself. He definitely had a grip on matters and was ready to do his first independent deal. In 1991, trouble brewed between his father and his partner, as the business was growing and Sarogi was unable to garner enough money for the business to meet the demand. Sarogi had been like a father figure to Jitu and had taught him accounting. That year turned out to be an unforgettable one for Jitu. At twenty-eight, he watched as the dispute widened ties between his father and his partner. At the same time, Mohandas decided to stop developing properties in Bengaluru. Completely distressed, Jitu explained to his father that his partner would survive while they would not, as real estate had become their bread and butter.

In 1993, Anant Sanghvi, a Gujarati landowner, sold Jitu a property on Infantry Road for Rs 1.6 crore. There Jitu developed his first office block, Embassy Point. Jitu held the deal down by giving Anantbhai Rs 25 lakh that he had borrowed from two friends. The place was a bit remotely located. He was lucky enough to sell two floors to Vikram Kirloskar for his company, Mysore Kirloskars. Jitu thus managed to recover the money even before the project was completed. Also, he made friends with Vikram Kirloskar, a relationship that has lasted close to three decades.

While he was closing the deal with the Kirloskars, on a return flight on their private jet from Pune, Jitu happened to meet D.L. Mirchandani, the VP of Kirloskar Engines and ended up selling a whole floor of the same building to him. Jitu still had an ace up his sleeve. He made Anantbhai a further offer: 'Do not take this money from me, become my partner and we will share the spoils. We will be 50-50 partners, and I will give you 50 per cent of the area free against your land price.' But Anantbhai was not impressed with the proposition, since not even autorickshaws ventured to that area. But Jitu persisted: 'What if I told you that I can sell the whole property?' So Anantbhai told him that if he did so, he might reconsider and reinvest the money. That was when Jitu broke the good news to him that he had only one floor left to sell.

This started a lasting friendship. Consequently, Anantbhai became Jitu's partner in the next few deals. Jitu ended up buying another piece of land, Embassy Square, from Anantbhai, which was successfully sold. From then on, Anantbhai became a sort of a mentor to Jitu.

He continued to invest in Jitu's projects, which, by now, also had many Hong Kong investors. Jitu went on to buy Shyam Prakash hotel, next to Embassy Square, which is now Embassy Icon. He paid Rs 54 crore for it, a big investment in 1996. Back at Embassy Point, Vikram Kirloskar now wanted to sell his floor space since there were financial problems in Mysore Kirloskar. Jitu got him an investor from Oman, who rented it out to Oracle (their first office in India). It turned out to be a win-win situation.

In 1992, Jitu's career took a different turn when architect
Naresh Venkatram asked him to meet the CMD of Reckitt
& Colman for a property on Bannerghatta Road on the
outskirts of Bengaluru. Virwani was confused about buying
10 acres on the outskirts, unsure if people would buy so far
away from the city. But Naresh asked him to just go along for
the ride. Jitu knew he did not have the money for the deal,
but he went anyway. He promptly fell in love with the land
when he saw it, imagining the project in his mind.

Jitu went home with a gleam in his eye. He knew he could
turn the property into a dreamland, but was still unsure of
taking on such a large property, which seemed totally out of his
reach. Selling at Rs 175 per sq. ft, it was worth Rs 7.62 crore,
a gold mine in his view. The chairman of Reckitt & Colman
asked to see him again for breakfast. Strangely, they wanted
to sell only to him, among all the people they had met. That
was when Jitu told them he did not have the money and
that they could sell to Southern Investments instead. But the
chairman asked him to reconsider and to make an offer with
payment terms this time. Mohandas was livid when he heard
about this, but Jitu could not let the property go as he was
now sure that he could pull it off.

He churned the numbers feverishly in his head. Most
private moneylenders lent at 24 per cent but he could easily
get money at 18 per cent from someone he knew, and even
if the land cost went up by Rs 15 per sq. ft every year, they
could make returns that would cover their interest costs.
Jitu was sure they would ultimately rake in the profits. His
calculating Sindhi mind could put any computer to shame.
His business team till today vouches for the same. He worked
the numbers carefully and made a plan based on a loan with

interest and a five-year payment schedule. Anantbhai, on Jitu's recommendation, also found himself buying 20 per cent equity in the property.

Despite all this, Mohandas was still upset that Jitu was buying something so far away from the city and saw no sense in it. But Jitu knew better and he felt he was at the right place at the right time with this one. Here he's quick to add that he believes the harder a person works the luckier he gets. To keep striving towards ones goal is what ultimately works. In the meantime, the fight between Mohandas and Sarogi reached a crescendo. Mohandas believed Sarogi was no longer an asset to the company. But Jitu thought otherwise; he felt Sarogi could be useful in the future in many ways.

Soon the Reckitt & Colman deal got even better for Jitu, because around the same time, in 1993, the Supreme Court passed an order that no urban land clearance would be given in the country. That worked in his favour, as he didn't have to pay anything to Reckitt & Colman till the law was relaxed. That bought him some time. All the developers were royally stuck, and since Jitu did not have the money, he waited till the land appreciated by 50 per cent that year. By 1994, the real estate boom arrived. Property prices skyrocketed, and soon Jitu's land, worth Rs 7 crore, valued at Rs 40 crore.

Soon afterwards, Jitu met Sajjan Jindal, who at the time had a public issue out for his company, JVSL. He was looking for a partner and wanted to invest close to Rs 200 crore in real estate. Jitu offered him his Reckitt & Colman property, now worth Rs 40 crore. Jitu wanted this deal to be done differently from how his father conducted his deals. He owed Reckitt & Colman Rs 5 crore, having already paid them

Rs 2.5 crore. He realized that if he sold only 50 per cent of the property for Rs 20 crore, he would still have Rs 15 crore in hand. That was a lot of money in hand for a thirty-year-old in 1996.

But Sajjan was adamant, saying, 'We are the Jindals and we like to own everything 100 per cent, but we will give you a working 20 per cent share for managing the project.' The argument started making sense to Jitu; he agreed to sell 100 per cent but wanted nothing to do with the project after that. Jitu had no interest in being a white-collar executive, but Sajjan understood that he needed Jitu in the loop, so he upped the percentage to 30. Finally Jitu agreed, and the deal was struck.

At the same time, Sarogi surrendered his 30 per cent share in the property by claiming interest on his investment. But one other partner of the Embassy Group chickened out and sold his 10 per cent share to Jitu, who offered it to an investor from Hong Kong, Mr Makhija, for Rs 210 crore, assuring him that he would one day sell the same for Rs 300 crore. Eventually, Jitu got him Rs 330 crore for it.

Around the same time, in 1993, Ravi Thambu Chetty, a friend of Jitu's and grandson of the diwan of Mysore, taught Jitu a lot about deal-making. Once they were chatting over lunch about starting a joint venture, (a project that went on to become Embassy Woods), when Jitu realized that Ravi was interested in Embassy properties. Jitu drove Ravi around, and the latter showed an interest in buying the ground floor of Embassy Point. Jitu needed Rs 2.5 crore, and he quoted exactly that amount and not the actual price of Rs 0.75 crore at which he was planning to sell the space to L. Sunderdas jewellers.

As luck would have it, Ravi agreed to Jitu's price. So Jitu exchanged with him a joint venture in Embassy Woods against the Embassy Point ground floor. It was from Ravi Thambu Chetty that Jitu actually learnt the game of leasing out office space. Until then Jitu had only been a seller. He felt that if he started offering bigger spaces and giving the tenants a large supply of electricity (150 kw per floor), he could easily be the guy they needed.

In the meantime, the Jindals went through a crisis and wanted to sell their property. They spoke to Jitu in a demeaning tone, referring to him as their manager . . . exactly what he had feared. This did not go down well with Jitu as he did not like the idea of working under anybody, let alone be treated like this. Since he did not have the funds to buy out the Jindals, he offered them flats in this Embassy building in return for the property.

Jitu still smiles every time he passes Jindal House on Peddar Road, Mumbai, since it reminds him of the Jindal deal. He learnt his lessons well in the school called life, sometimes from his mistakes and sometimes from people. But being a true Sindhi at heart, he refused to get hoodwinked by anybody. As the business grew, Jitu watched the real estate world evolve from the sidelines with the keenest eye.

Jitu's Management Style

Rajesh Bajaj, current president of corporate affairs at the Embassy Group, has known Jitu for twenty-five years. It is Rajesh who makes the decisions at the group when Jitu is unavailable. He says Jitu has a mind that works 24x7, noting just about everything about everything. Even when a near-flawless presentation is made, says Rajesh, Jitu sits through it without a word and then comes up with his own view on the matter, pointing out that one thing that might be missing or wrong.

Jitu is clearly a man who gives a lot to the people he loves, but he has over the years learnt to keep away from pressure and from people who give it to others. He is a man who likes to be on top of things, be it a situation, a deal or even a relationship. He is known to be just and level-headed, even if that means hurting himself financially.

All this Jitu learnt from his father, who, he says, had a distinct way of conducting business and treating his customers. Though he was firm about his pricing, he would intermittently grant some discounts. Jitu truly believes that in real estate, if one sells with a good heart, everybody involved prospers. Jitu's business mantra has always been to forgive and to move on, and he has lived it out clearly in most of his relationships.

Daulat Chhabria, a freelancer/top realtor who has worked with and known Jitu for over twenty years, praises Jitu for his integrity. Jitu is known to be a risk-taker who fully understands the loans he takes on. He prefers to borrow rather than to invest his own money. Because of his commitment and strong sense of responsibility, his investors have been dedicated to him.

Jitu is also known to share profits with his staff. Every three years he treats his entire staff—right from the driver to the senior-most executive—to a foreign holiday; the company makes sure they all have their passports in order. The group started out with seventy-four employees and now has 350. Jitu's mission is to reward everybody the same for their work, a principle applied even during the annual Diwali party and in the gifts given to all by the Embassy Group.

Key Business Deals

Over time, Jitu began to be known as a prolific dealmaker because he was clearly able to see the inherent patterns in business and people. This made him see value in deals and properties where others couldn't, giving him the first-mover advantage. Some people also nicknamed him 'land whisperer' and with good reason.

But luck did not favour Jitu every time. In 1990, he bought a large property from the Chowgules for Rs 6.75 crore, signing an MOU for Rs 67.5 lakh. For this he applied for a loan to Vijaya Bank. Sadhanand Shetty, the bank's chairman at the time, promised he would find funds for the group from the Unit Trust of India (UTI). Embassy Group paid the MOU amount and agreed to pay the rest of the money in eighteen months' time. When the Jagdish Tytler scam broke and Sadhanand was implicated in it, he resigned, leaving them at the mercy of the new chairman, A. K. Shetty, who saw them merely as Sadhanand's customers and not as Vijaya Bank's customers.

He said the bank would lend them Rs 4 crore for further business if they returned the money they had borrowed. Trusting him, they did so, but the chairman went back on his word. Jitu was stumped. He closed all his thirty-eight accounts in Vijaya Bank thereafter. The Embassy Group then took its business to Federal Bank and paid back the Chowgules with the sale of some other properties.

Construction started on the property that was to become The Embassy. But due to political turmoil (the Rajiv Gandhi assassination), the rupee fell from 17 to 33 to the dollar. With the economy being down, The Embassy sold only 100,000 sq. ft out of 250,000 sq. ft. Around the same time, Jitu met a rich businessman from Abu Dhabi who was in the medical services business, and was interested in buying. But instead of the deal falling into place after all the documentation was done, the businessman retracted on the figures he had agreed to. Thinking he had failed yet again, Jitu felt angry and heavy-hearted. But as luck would have it, the winds changed, and within two months he was able to command his price again as property prices began to soar, moving from Rs 1,050 per sq. ft to Rs 3,000 per sq. ft, allowing Jitu to make a killing in 1993. He laughed all the way to the bank, and the group was cash-rich again.

Since Jitu had no projects in line now, he began to invest in office space in all the other builders' buildings, because office space was becoming important in the scheme of things. Along with his chartered accountant, Gopi Krishnan, who was initially his marketing person, he changed the whole game. Jitu with his strategy and Gopi with his Excel sheets conquered the 1994–1996 boom. What they bought for Rs 1,800 per sq. ft they sold for Rs 3,500 per sq. ft, and what they bought for Rs 3,000 per sq. ft, they sold at Rs 5,500 per sq. ft. The group was now able to call the shots on the pricing index.

Expanding his office space holdings, Jitu then bought four floors next to Manipal Centre in The Estate. The money put in consisted of both Embassy money and investments from Hong Kong investors. They sold it at double the buying rate of Rs 1,800 per sq. ft. At one point, the Prestige group and the Embassy Group were competing for a property that belonged to a church. Every time the bidding price rose the

church stood to benefit, so Mohandas asked Jitu to surrender
the deal. The property stood opposite Bishop Cotton School,
and cost Rs 12 crore. But instead of surrendering, Jitu struck
a deal with Irfan Razack (of Prestige) and took 20 per cent
of the built-up area, thereby forging a friendship between the
two competitors.

During that time Jitu also encouraged and helped many
Hong Kong buyers by selling to them at the same price that
he bought property at, taking only half the money from them.
When they sold, he took 20 per cent as service fee. Since the
deal was as transparent as that, the investors got to make money.

The Fall

In 1996, there arose a situation of no buyers in the market,
leading to a cash flow problem. Jitu agrees that he was not
smart enough to see it coming. The group had created a huge
market where there was now a sudden glut of investors. It was
then natural that they were headed for disaster. The banks at
the time were still kind to the group, standing right by it. The
only debt Jitu had was of Rs 12 crore with the Federal Bank;
one that had accumulated as they offered him Rs 4 crore a
year, every March. But the good thing was that every time he
got that money he would go land shopping.

When the crash happened, Jitu realized that his debt
had been growing like a black hole (it had accumulated to
Rs 37 crore finally). So he decided to change his strategy
immediately. As land prices dipped, bank interests rose,
and the situation took Jitu quite by surprise as he had all
along been riding the wave of growth. While he became a
workaholic trying to save his business, his personal life was

crumbling in more ways than one. It didn't spare his family either. It eroded the walls of trust among them and everybody started questioning his integrity.

Jitu felt his anger building up at the injustice of the situation. He faced it single-handedly, but eventually it resulted in his separation from his family. All his dreams of having a successful family-run business came crashing around him, and things were never the same again.

Jitu settled his debts with the bank, selling off property to meet the mortgages. He dealt with the cash flow problem; being the only one in the company who knew the money maze, only he could put the puzzle back together and pull the company out of trouble. Luckily, no money had ever been spent on luxuries, holidays or expensive cars, and it was all accounted for.

This claim was endorsed by Narpat Singh Choraria, a Marwari who had looked after all the family money during the days (1985–1996) of Jitu's father but moved with Jitu and is now one of the directors of the Embassy Group. He rules with the same iron hand as he did earlier, except that the numbers now are bigger. Jitu remembers the time when even the money spent on coffee used to be scrutinized. Narpatji is Jitu's senior who helps in decision-making for the group now. He says Jitu's brain is like a super computer, and is surprised at his intuitiveness that works like a sixth sense.

The Final Settlement

Looking back, Jitu realized that it probably looked as if he had raced ahead of everybody else. Jealousy had turned out to be a hard taskmaster. Others thought he was replacing the old guard. At one point, his lawyer, Anup Shah, warned him that nobody would want to do business with him if he had so many cases against him, filed by family itself.

Jitu set to work on the reconciliation diligently. He did not read even one of the cases his family had filed against him, knowing fully well that that might change his mind about them. Not being able to stomach what might happen to him if he stayed any longer in the warring zone with his brother and father, Jitu decided to let go and start his career all over again. With his mind all made up, Jitu went to his father's home and asked for a final settlement.

He promised himself that if the settlement happened, he would shave his head at the shrine of Tirupati Balaji. Jitu wanted to offer his father and brother the first choice of properties, and was ready to give them Embassy Heights, but his father wanted a farm that Jitu had bought, assuming that it was the best property they owned. They had a family lunch to seal their choices, but their arbitrator came back and told them their choices were bad. So they resumed talks. Finally, Jitu was left with Rs 18 crore less and all the debts. He also got all the land on the outskirts of the city which was parcelled off as junk.

Mohandas also made an offer to Jitu to leave everything behind and start afresh elsewhere, debt-free and with Rs 15 crore, but Jitu refused to take the money and walk away from everything. He felt the investors were his responsibility, and if he left the real estate business he would be cheating them. Having made that decision he sleeps easy even to this day because he feels his conscience is clean.

Jitu's knowledge of the real estate business has always been his treasure, and that was another reason to not leave it.

The settlement took three years, from 1996 to 1999, to get done. Jitu then started all over again, with his Rs 18 crore-deficit account. The family had asked three friends to be the final arbitrators. When Jitu left, he told everyone, 'We are parting ways for reasons best known to us'. Seventy-four out of seventy-eight people in Embassy followed him to the new company.

In those three years, the Federal Bank interest increased from Rs 17 crore to more than Rs 37 crore. All the construction work had come to a standstill as the family was busy fighting the legal cases. A.T. Gopinath, the CFO of the group, is today part of Jitu's inner circle; he has been so since the time he made the choice to move with Jitu. Rajesh Bajaj, Gopi Krishnan and Narpatji also moved with him.

Jitu allowed a more democratic way of working, delegated wisely, and, though known to be extremely calculating, was straightforward too. He set standards for his co-workers in such a way that when he defined what he wanted, they complied, knowing fully well that they were being given a long rope. He promoted ingenuity, but always made the final call. His belief was that the glass was always full, and if it wasn't at any point, well, then there was an opportunity to fill it. His strength was definitely the relationship he shared with his people.

Start of a New Decade

Gopi Bhawnani of RSP Architects, Planners and Engineers, an architectural firm, speaks well and admiringly of Jitu, whom he has helped with building designs, planning and engineering since 1994. He says Jitu is a man who thrives on relationships and runs a lean operation, and though he appears to delegate, he controls everything with his final decisions.

By the end of the decade, Jitu was on the lookout for new market trends since he had somewhat exhausted opportunities on the residential building front. He was now waiting and watching, to see how to take his business in another direction. He knew he had the manpower, the know-how and the reputation. All he needed was to make the right move in the right direction, first fully understanding the market. Many Western companies had already started using India as an offshoring base.

When Jitu was starting all over again, a man called Sanjay Ghodawat of Star Gutka came into his life. He invested huge sums of money with Jitu. A silent kind of person, Sanjay gave him seed capital of Rs 130 crore to rebuild his business. Sanjay has remained in Jitu's life and keeps reinvesting with him. Today he is one of his friends and their families have become close too.

Around the same time, Jitu noticed that large Indian IT companies were setting up their own office parks to meet their needs. They had to be insulated from the hustle and bustle of city life; they needed landscaped gardens, round-the-clock power supply; and wanted to offer their employees a choice of eateries and facilities like gymnasiums, hotels, theatres and yoga rooms.

Companies were taking steps to expand their operations by significantly increasing their staff strength. For instance, Microsoft had moved from hiring 1,000 employees a year to 5,000 a year. This meant more office space was needed almost immediately. Jitu crunched some numbers and worked it out at Rs 100 a sq. ft per employee, Microsoft would need 500,000 sq. ft of office space. But the statistics had also shown earlier that no company had invested more than 100,000 sq. ft at one go.

Now was definitely the time for change, with IBM, Microsoft, Fidelity Investment and DaimlerChrysler spearheading it. But, of course, it came with their global policy of not allowing purchase of office space in India.

So the next best thing was to lease office parks. If the group wanted to cater to these companies, they would need to offer state-of-the-art office spaces, with an owner and a property manager to take care of maintenance needs. This is where the Embassy Group carved its niche. It did not merely develop and lease out but also maintained its properties.

In the days when Jitu had recently set up on his own, he was still not considered to be in the big league of builders. But he bridged that gap as he went on to do a joint venture with K.J. George, who is today the infrastructure minister in Bengaluru. Jitu had a knack for sniffing out great properties. His daring and quick decisions got him prime buys. In 1993–94, Jitu and K.J. George had been doing business and knew each other well. Years later, George happened to have a 5-acre property in Bengaluru, for which he wanted Jitu to make an access road. Jitu gave him Rs 50 lakh towards this on a temporary basis. This did not materialize, and, finally, George insisted that Jitu develop a project on the same land.

So Jitu ventured to make Embassy Golf Links in a joint venture with George in 2002. It started as a mere 5-acre project, with ANZ InfoTech as an occupant. IBM signed on for 700,000 sq. ft on the same day as the *bhoomi pujan*. Knowing the market was going to go through the ceiling,

Jitu quickly bought more land, and Embassy Golf Links went on to become a 60-acre, 4.5 million sq. ft facility.

Out of the blue, another family, the Aroras of Tapasya Group from Delhi, wanted to buy a whole building from Jitu in Embassy Golf Links Business Park (2 lakh sq. ft). They still invest with the Embassy Group.

All of Jitu's deals are usually connected and often in exchange for more land than money. Though he had done all the work, Jitu felt he owed a lot to George because without him he would not have created the Golf Links space. Today, Embassy Golf Links Business Park is one of Jitu's finest creations. On its 60 acres stand twenty food courts and a Hilton hotel, among other facilities. It is a fully occupied and a busy workplace, with 43,000 employees on its premises.

Catering to a workforce of 100,000, the Embassy Manayata Business Park is easily one of India's largest business parks. It has a vast working campus that is situated on the Outer Ring Road in north Bengaluru, making it the only operational integrated project near the Kempegowda International Airport. Forty-three companies, such as ANZ, Cerner, Cognizant, Fidelity, IBM, Lowe's, Northern Trust, NSN and Target, can be found on this 110-acre workplace. It offers conveniences such as intra-city transportation and a sports zone.

Pune, being so close to Mumbai, was the next obvious choice for Jitu for expansion in real estate. Close to the Mumbai-Pune Expressway, the Embassy Techzone enjoys easy accessibility to Mumbai, the country's economic capital. It has all the features that award-winning parks do, which makes it a world-class facility. It is a property of 68 acres and has a total developable potential of 4.4 million sq. ft of office space. An SEZ claims 50 acres, while the rest is dedicated to various non-SEZ activities.

Running such a large office park can be a logistics nightmare, but the group has worked hard at perfecting it. It remains the preferred partner for customers, even after they have done multiple deals. Not quite stopping there, the group has further extended its plans and execution to a services company that provides housekeeping and maintenance services.

Jitu's style of doing business has changed over time. For instance, when he worked with the Garg brothers of Vrindavan Technology Park, who had an excellent property of 106 acres, the value of land was pretty high, and Jitu had to employ a completely different strategy from his usual methods. Jitu needed presence on the Outer Ring Road, and this was just the place. Many companies, such as Accenture, GICs, RMZ and even Blackstone, had tried to do business with Vrindavan but had failed. That only encouraged Jitu, as he has always liked a chase and enjoyed challenges. He decided to buy the property and approached Blackstone for the capital. Blackstone agreed, but only once all the details were finalized and all the Garg brothers had agreed to sell.

This proved to be a very difficult job, but over time Jitu got two of the brothers to sell. One cashed out while the other stayed on with the project and became a partner. The last Garg brother turned out to be the toughest. He was very insecure, threw tantrums and delayed the project. Through it all, Jitu humoured him endlessly, spending time with him and his family, bringing him around finally. That was when Jitu informed Tuhin Parikh, senior managing director of Blackstone, that they could go ahead.

When they had to settle on a price, Jitu agreed to what the brothers were asking for without a fuss. He decided it was better to keep them happy than to bargain with them. Negotiating would have got Jitu the land for Rs 25–30 crore less, but he decided he would rather do business with them and retain their friendship since he was in it for the long run. He felt the bargaining would rankle them and they would feel cheated.

So Jitu showed them a 'non-Sindhi' attitude by agreeing immediately. But he also knew that he had done the very Sindhi thing by thinking long term. The brothers were totally sold on Jitu's tactic, and that's when they gave him control of everything, including the negotiations with Blackstone.

Jitu had also locked in the property by buying the Garg brothers' management company, Assets, for Rs 100 crore and becoming their 20 per cent partner in their main company. At one point the same company had been available to Jitu for Rs 35-40 crore, but his CEO, Gopinath, hadn't quite seen the sense in buying it.

Once all the Garg brothers were convinced to sell, Blackstone decided to come in as an investor. Jitu pumped in Rs 350 crore of his own money, which he had never done earlier. Blackstone only wanted an 18 per cent stake in the project. But Jitu was thinking way ahead. To him, getting 106 acres of land in one piece right in the city was a rare thing, and if somebody like Flipkart rented 3 million sq. ft, he knew he would make a killing. Jitu knew very well that equity is not based on land value but mainly on rental value.

Tuhin recognized that Jitu's way of working was to relentlessly pursue a matter till he got what he wanted. If he found the client to be straightforward, he would do everything in his power to engage him, but if somebody tried to browbeat or bully him, he would make sure to pay him back in the same coin.

This acquisition was then called Embassy Tech Village, the single largest private business park in the heart of the city. It has four buildings where 19,000 knowledge workers are employed; 1.9 million sq. ft of office space has been created; and 3.8 million sq. ft more remains to be built. This mammoth development has commercial, retail and residential components. Its tenants are Cisco, Great-West Financial, KPMG, Seagate, Sears, Software AG, Sony-Wells Fargo and Quest. It was developed with green initiatives and won the MIPIM Asia Green Building Award and the Best Environmental Friendly Commercial Project at Realty Plus Excellence Awards in 2014.

HDFC

A State Bank of India official once advised Jitu that bank relationships are a must because banks are the 'people who build people'. When Jitu took on the Embassy Golf Links project, he approached ING Vyasa for a loan since its managing director stayed in Embassy Woods. They offered Rs 25 crore, which HDFC Bank countered with Rs 40 crore.

His tryst with Deepak Parekh, chairman of HDFC, India's leading housing finance company, started at that time. Deepak, a Padma Bhushan awardee, says Jitu's reputation as a smart developer precedes him. His quality of construction is very good, as is evident from his Golf Links property. Early on, Deepak found Jitu aggressive, but believed he would change as he grew older, but that was not the case. Jitu has only become much more aggressive and ambitious, jokes Deepak.

Deepak still thinks Jitu should not take such big risks, as large products over a long time frame can be worrisome, especially because the world we live in right now is uncertain and times are unpredictable. Every IT back office company is worried about its survival because of Trump. Jitu's diversification out of Bengaluru, into Hyderabad, Chennai and Pune, has been good, and he has shown that he is a true entrepreneur, willing to take greater risks as he grows. Jitu's track record as a good borrower has prompted HDFC Bank to sanction more and more loans to him. But no amount of persuasion from Deepak, asking him to slow down, has had an impact on Jitu.

According to the HDFC chairman, Jitu's business is 70–80 per cent commercial, and some portion residential. Deepak says, 'In order to capture the Indian potential, he will have to build more affordable homes because they are the future of India, since the government in this budget has also given proper incentives for affordable homes. The demand is insatiable, and the shortages are huge.' His advice to Jitu would be to go the Tata, Godrej and Mahindra way, since even they have started building affordable housing. The government has also made the first five years of construction tax-free, and affordable housing is aided by policies such as the Pradhan Mantri Awas Yojana.

According to Deepak, real estate in the commercial space is definitely going to slow down, whether one likes it or not, going by the common trend one sees right now. Even big companies, who used to hire between 20,000 and 30,000 employees every year, have started hiring only 10,000–15,000 in 2017. Things are going to change drastically when Trump finishes dealing with North Korea, Russia and Mexico and his trade pacts, his fighting of tax reductions and Obama-care, and turns his sights to Asia, particularly India.

Diversification

Jitu likes keeping his tenants happy, and is known to go the extra mile for them. To manage this side of the business, the group started Embassy Services in 1993, which he has entrusted to a loyal friend, Pradeep Nenumal Lala, who is the CEO. It is Embassy's own professional property management division, which improves rental values and continues to enhance the long-term commitment of the group to its projects. This company manages everything from housekeeping and maintenance to organizing buses and running crèches across 20 million sq. ft of IT parks, commercial and residential spaces across the country, in cities such as Bengaluru, Chennai, Pune and Noida.

Backed by a team of 100 core employees, aided by 3,000 others to whom work has been outsourced, Embassy Services is today an independent company worth Rs 500 crore. It provides the same services to other developers too. People vouch for the fact that it meets international standards. This is the country's first company offering property management to have three ISO certifications.

Plans were set up for individual hotels to be built on each Embassy property for tenants and visitors. Embassy Hospitality was created for this purpose. A retired old friend of Jitu's, Sartaj Singh, agreed to be the president of this company. Sartaj comments that Jitu surrounds himself with friends so that he can work with them as colleagues and place immense trust in every working relationship. He calls Jitu 'a Sindhi with the heart of a sardar'.

Michael Holland, Embassy's CEO of commercial spaces, has always found Jitu very compelling. He feels Jitu has always had a certain amount of business pragmatism, reaching out to people first and bridging differences, if any, later.

Synergy

Sankey Prasad and Tuhin Parekh of Blackstone had been colleagues at TCG Real Estate. In 2002, Sankey built two of the first buildings in Golf Links for Embassy. When his project management company, Synergy, was being sold in 2003, he asked Jitu to buy it. Jitu knew that Sankey had done a good job, and knew fully well he would need Synergy for all his further businesses. He agreed to buy it. He was offered a 70 per cent stake in it, and the sellers kept 30 per cent for themselves. Jitu invested Rs 25 lakh with them and another Rs 50 lakh for expanding the company. Sankey continued working for Jitu.

A year later, when the company wanted to announce a dividend, Sankey decided to dilute his 30 per cent stake among some new professionals. Jitu felt that if this happened he would not have much skin in the game, so he told Sankey not to deal with his heart but with his mind. Exactly a year later, Synergy brought in Tuhin Parekh to buy 35 per cent equity in the company and asked Jitu if he would be willing to sell 20 per cent for Rs 30 crore. He agreed. Jitu remains a shareholder in Synergy to date, but does not sit in on board meetings.

Over time, Sankey has become an integral part of Embassy. Jitu strongly believes that his success has been due to Embassy's staff, RSP's designs and Synergy's ability to build.

Blackstone

Blackstone as a company is always on the lookout for opportunities for risk-adjusted returns. It set up in India in 2007, when there was a real estate boom in the country. Since everything was overpriced, the company was slow to invest, but it liked Sankey Prasad's Synergy, whose biggest client at the time was Embassy. That's how Blackstone was introduced to Jitu, who was just getting out of his family feud and knew precious little about building office spaces.

What they liked about Jitu as a builder was that he had moved away from the old ways of working, which would have everything in-house. Instead, Jitu ventured out, spending all his energy to find the right piece of land, choosing the right customers and keeping them happy. That was why his partnership with Synergy happened.

Blackstone reconnected with Jitu in 2011, when Jitu mentioned that he needed funding for his project, Embassy Terraces. Tuhin Parikh, the senior managing director, liked that particular piece of land and agreed that Blackstone would invest Rs 130 crore. When Blackstone exited, they did so with good returns, but in between they worked with Jitu on other projects too. They reconnected again when Jitu brought up the matter of the 11-million-sq-ft Embassy Manyata Tech Park, from which HDFC wanted to exit. Both Tuhin and Jitu have always connected over numbers, so Tuhin met with him in Singapore and struck the deal.

Soon afterwards, in 2012, Blackstone and Jitu joined hands to form an equal joint venture, Embassy Office Parks. The rent from the office parks in the property was enough to take care of the interest costs. Embassy Office Parks currently consists of four office parks and is aiming to take the rental income up to Rs 1,300 crore in the next two years, from Rs 48 per sq. ft to Rs 70 per sq. ft.

Jitu's ambition and Blackstone's appetite to invest more have always gelled well. Blackstone knows Jitu's deals are complicated, but it appreciates that he always makes an effort to keep them transparent. Tuhin says about Jitu, 'He understands risk well, and even knows how much of it he should be taking.' They always keep their eyes open for the next deal to go into together.

In 2015, Tuhin brought in the Four Seasons deal, which was in trouble with Goldman Sachs, with the landowner and also with the banks. It was a messy deal, with an abandoned site that was actually underwater, and on which even the contractors had walked out. But Jitu was by now known for his knack of cleaning up messy deals. He had somehow figured out how he could tap into the highest value of any project.

Tuhin says, 'What I personally like about Jitu is that he has figured out in life what his strengths and weaknesses are, so much so that he collects all kinds of loyal people around him who grow with him, while he primarily focuses only on what he does best.'

Blackstone says of Embassy today: 'In Embassy we found a partner who is willing to embrace challenges and newer ideas, keep striving for excellence and taking joint decisions for overall value creation for the stakeholders.' The last five years have been very good for Embassy as a group, simply because Jitu moved to developing office spaces while the whole industry was struggling. Since the group has tied up with Blackstone, it has witnessed remarkable traction in its portfolio.

Now both Blackstone and Embassy are ready to merge their portfolios in a real estate investment trust (REIT) and take it public.

REIT

One would imagine that Jitu has his plate full, but this self-proclaimed workaholic is now setting up a REIT which acts as a vehicle for investments in real estate. The Embassy Office Parks REIT, a JV between Blackstone PE and the Embassy Group, is likely to materialize in 2018. It is the first REIT in India, one of the largest in Asia (with over 35 million sq. ft of grade A commercial office space) and is expected to set a high benchmark for others. This is also another way for Jitu to consolidate his office portfolio under one vehicle which will continue to undertake large office parks and ensure the groups' expansion is fuelled by tax-free dividends.

REITs have the potential to create a virtuous cycle of lower finance cost, increased liquidity, higher employment, and act as catalysts for commercial real estate growth. Additionally, they serve as an excellent and alternate investment option (other than traditional gold and residences etc.) for investors by providing regular dividends, capital appreciation and more importantly to be a part of the Indian commercial real estate growth story.

Stonehill International School

Jitu's home and riding school sit on a 400-acre property beside Stonehill International School, in which he has invested over Rs 100 crore, 2008 onwards. It is an Embassy Group education initiative, managed by Vikram Shah, the chairperson of the governing council of the school. Shaina Ganpathy, the GM of corporate affairs at the group, is also involved in the school. Vikram has known Jitu for some time now; he says that in spite of real estate being a pretty murky business, his dealings with Jitu have always been straightforward.

Stonehill, built on 45 acres and developed in consultation with the CIS (Council of International Schools) is among the select schools in India that offer all three international baccalaureate programmes, supported by outstanding facilities. It has an early childhood centre, a primary years programme, a middle years programme, a diploma course, and even offers college placement. Apart from this, there are facilities for the creative arts, extra-curricular activities, physical education and sports.

CSR

Municipal Schools

The Embassy Group has adopted fifteen government schools, transforming the lives of over 4,000 children. The goal is to eventually adopt thirty-six government schools. Jitu has taken it on himself to adopt these schools to help the government introduce good teachers into the system.

The group has also adopted the Tarahunise village school and has completely rebuilt it. It is in the same area as Stonehill International School; it is now called Stonehill Government Higher Secondary School. The more privileged children put in hours of community service at this school. Embassy Group provides the students uniforms, clean study areas and also midday meals. Understanding the needs of the children, the group has made sure they have separate rooms for meals, a library, classrooms, a staff room, a headmaster's room and clean toilets.

To ensure that they match the other schools, the group has provided sports equipment for table tennis, cricket, football and volleyball at this village school. Collaboration with an NGO, Colours of Life (run by Simran Chandok), has only enhanced the progress of this school project. Shaina Ganapathy adds that the group shares the same vision as this NGO and aims to take this relationship forward to ensure that all the schools in the area get the same support.

Today the village school has English learning programmes, art classes, supplementary maths classes, yoga summer camps, and even computer classes. For the student, all this makes for a holistic approach to learning. Shaina is of the opinion that instead of giving them just uniforms, books and stationery, 'we realize that we should give them programmes that will make the children worthy of employment later.' While the Embassy Group is building vast technological parks and Bengaluru's most advanced residences, they are also building lives and actually being the change they want to see.

The Riding School

In 1996, there were rumours of an airport being built near Bengaluru, which led to many people buying land around the proposed area. Understanding the situation sooner than the rest, Jitu started buying land parcels on the Devanahalli Road. He invested in 250 acres which became the Embassy International Riding School.

It was around this time he bought a farm from a Mr. Ruia for Rs 7.96 crore. At the time, Ruia had Silva Storai—the only woman jockey to have won two Derbies in succession—as a tenant on his farm, along with her two horses. Ruia introduced Jitu and Silva, which started a friendship between the two as they shared a keen interest in horses. Jitu laughs when he thinks of the days when Silva would pay him Rs 1,000 for the two stables that she occupied and wondered what kind of a return on investment it was from the land that he had just bought for $2 million. Today she is his close friend and runs the riding school for him as a working partner.

Completely comfortable in her stables, Silva remarks that Jitu is very loyal and gives his colleagues enough space to take their own decisions. Though their wavelengths matched, as colleagues they have raved and ranted alternatively but always had the same vision in mind. It was Silva who introduced the idea of starting a riding school on that land, on which Jitu himself learnt to ride. Architects from Singapore made designs, and it was named the Embassy Ranch. Buying designs all those years ago from architect Andy Fischer, Jitu did not realize that he would make his home there later.

Horses were trained and some ex-racehorses were also bought. Memberships started pouring in. People came to network while they rode or to introduce their children to a new sport. Today the riding school has eighty horses and ponies and also breeds race horses.

The riding school, which began as nothing, suddenly became a brand for the Embassy Group. There was a time when Embassy was losing money. People would wonder how the owner lived on a 200-acre farm and owned a riding school if the company was in trouble. The riding school appeared to advertise the stability of Embassy. Jitu had actually grown up surrounded by horse racing and gambling in the family, but he has since then turned the activity around into one that is not so destructive as the picture of his early memories.

Jitu encourages sports such as eventing, dressage and showjumping by sponsoring four participants who are being trained to compete in the Asian Games. He sponsored three in the last Asian Games. Young adults are also being trained in England and Germany, where he has fourteen horses. He proudly says, 'I'm trying to build the sport single-handedly in the country. I am not looking for land or benefits from the government.' His dream has always been to convert part of the land into a club and focus on world-class riding facilities for showjumping, making the sport more affordable for good riders.

Logistics, Warehousing, Solar Power

The Embassy Group has come a long way from its early days, but is also ready for its next phase of growth. *If we are to go by any of the numbers projected in consumption growth in the e-commerce sector ($15 billion) and the FMCG sector ($49 billion), 14 per cent growth in GDP in the manufacturing sector, 8 per cent contribution to the total global agricultural output, 10 million tonnes of estimated shortage in the cold storage sector and 30 per cent wastage of harvest, then we realize the quantum of warehousing services that is required in the country. To bridge the need for warehousing space, Embassy has started developing warehouses in seven key cities across India—Ahmedabad, Bengaluru, Chennai, Delhi NCR, Hyderabad, Mumbai and Pune.

The group has acquired 52 acres of industrial land, strategically located in Chakan/Pune (with development potential of 1.1 million sq. ft), 300 acres in Bhiwandi/Mumbai (with development potential of 6.5 million sq. ft), and 150 acres in Delhi NCR (with development potential of 3 million sq. ft).

It has already acquired 198 acres in Sriperumbudur (off Chennai) for two industrial parks, with links to ports and airports. Factories will be set up for manufacturing needs, and 60 per cent of the space will be reserved for warehousing. Plans are afoot for acquiring more land parcels near Delhi.

Anshul Singhal, CEO of Embassy Industrial Parks, worked at JSW for seven years before joining Jitu. An absolute go-getter, he met Jitu while selling him a building in 2011–2012. Embassy Industrial Parks was created to take care of the burgeoning demand for modern industrial and warehousing space. Now, with a $250 million joint venture with an American private equity firm, Warburg Pincus, the funding of the project is to the tune of Rs 1,000 crore. It is FCPA (Foreign Corrupt Practices Act) compliant and there are plans to set up warehouses all over India, for which land has been acquired as described earlier. Embassy will put in Rs 1,600 crore and Warburg Pincus, $1 billion. Big names like Flipkart, Amazon, Snapdeal, ITC, Procter & Gamble and Unilever are part of the deal.

'A happy employee is not about the salary but all about empowerment, trust and treatment,' says Anshul. He is absolutely certain that his decision to move companies has been good because there is no one else who places so much trust in and gives so much freedom to his co-workers as Jitu. He admires Jitu in totality since he leads by example and is easy to do business with. Working seamlessly with people has indeed got Jitu the reputation that he enjoys today.

Personal Life

Jitu is a planner, as can be seen from how he has fashioned his life, taking his friends and family along. Embassy has no partners; he and his sons own it wholly. His children have a right over everything that belongs to him. Karan has already found his place in the sun, while Aditya is currently shadowing Jitu.

After his divorce, Jitu remarried. His new wife, Lina, is a Russian from Dubai. Natalie, their lovely twenty-year-old daughter is pursuing business studies in the UK. She is currently interning at the Embassy Group, learning the ropes from the ground level up. Some day she would like to join the hospitality industry. Neel, the youngest in the family, is away at university in the UK.

Lina lives partly in Dubai, but spends a lot of her time in Bengaluru, where she lives with Jitu on their 400-acre property. She is closely involved in Jitu's life and activities. Jitu had bought this plot of land in parts. Conveniently situated near the airport, this property was conceptualized in 2003. It was actually built in 2012 on 30 acres of land. A Sindhi mindset led Jitu to believe that if anything untoward ever happened to him, he would be able to give 10 acres each to his sons. Jitu has always ensured that his children remain safe, having seen that when families go through bad times some members get hurt more than the rest.

The Virwani Legacy

Mohandas always wanted to make good residential buildings, private clubs, hotels, and build a good name for the group. All this Jitu has succeeded in doing, almost like a trusted arm of his father. In the old days, fathers did not pay sons to work with them, at least initially, but today Jitu gives his sons good allowances, as he is aware that he is dealing with a completely different generation. Jitu in his time always had to work for the extra money he needed. With his father, Jitu felt work was relegated and not delegated to him. He felt he was just thrown into the deep end and had to learn not only to swim but to survive too. He elaborates: 'When you build people, those same people help you build a business!'

Talking about the glut in the market and what is going to be the future of real estate in India, he remarks that there is going to be a huge spillover that will move from Bengaluru to Hyderabad and then to Chennai. On the anvil are steel buildings and prefab buildings that will be put together like Lego pieces. A Middle Eastern company makes those in Krishnagiri, Tamil Nadu.

Another thing about Jitu is that he is particular about the quality of everything he does, and his buildings are proof of this trait of his. He swears by furbishing all his buildings after a gap of six or seven years, making sure their value remains high so that rents can be increased. Jitu has also started showing very stylish sample flats to customers even before the buildings are readied so that the customer gets a view of what is in store and is tempted to buy. For example, in one of his buildings where his flats are worth more than Rs 18 crore each, 200 flats have already been sold in sixty days. Jitu also keeps in mind that real estate is a cyclical industry.

He keeps a keen eye on everything, declaring that every decision he makes has a strong mathematical backing to it. This is evident in the way his businesses are managed. For instance, Embassy Services made Rs 80 crore last year, while Stonehill International School has its own reserves, which also provides the funds for the municipal school that he runs with the government. Similarly, the riding school has enhanced the value of the land his home is built on. Now, with a knowledge park coming up and the fact that he has improved accessibility by building a road worth Rs 45 crore through the land, its value has only escalated further.

Jitu is a firm believer in the statement, 'the difference between boys and men is the cost of their toys.' He definitely enjoys making money and does it for the thrill of the big deal, though he personally doesn't really need much of it. He believes in comfort, and dresses only in half-sleeved white and sky-blue custom-made shirts coupled with black, grey or navy blue trousers to work. Special events get him into readymade suits from either Canali or Ermenegildo Zegna.

The Embassy Group Today

Conversing with Jitu Virwani provides one a lot of insight into his life. He feels he has seen many upheavals, challenges and struggles in his life and career, often finding himself at a crossroads and being forced to make intuitive decisions. But all that has worked in his favour, as he has achieved more than just success in his endeavours; he says he has also achieved peace and happiness in good measure.

For the last three years, the Embassy Group has been streamlining itself by hiring heads for each of its key verticals—offices, residential and industrial parks—who will handle all day-to-day operations. He spends most of his time focusing on the larger trends and maintaining relationships with his stakeholders, tenants, land partners and financiers—a long list of people.

With an average of 34 million sq. ft being leased every year, the market is ready to accommodate another 300 million sq. ft in the next ten years. There are half a dozen companies in the market today that can provide this kind of real estate in the market: DLF, GIC, Brookfield, RMZ, Prestige and DivyaSree.

Jitu also recently bought the Le Meridien hotel in Bengaluru which his father had wanted to buy at one time from a Sindhi gentleman, Pardhnani. Jitu bought all the shares of the gentleman's publicly listed company, which has office spaces and a hotel in Cochin too. The gentlemen treated Jitu like a son and made it viable for him to buy the property.

In the hotel space, Embassy has also strengthened its partnership with the Hilton by signing a management agreement for one of the largest dual-branded hotels in India located in Embassy Manyata Business Park, featuring the Hilton Hotels and Resorts and the Garden Hilton brands, to be developed and owned by the Embassy Group and managed by the Hilton. This project is slated for completion in 2020.

In 2016, Bengaluru saw the launch of its largest integrated master-planned city, Embassy Springs, which is one of the latest offerings from the Embassy Group. It is a 300-acre integrated residential city in north Bengaluru, the new growth corridor of India's Silicon Valley and the epicentre of the real estate boom in the city. It lies 9 km from the new international airport with great road connectivity, what with an express highway running nearby and having close proximity to the Ring Road. There are plans for a monorail too.

It is home to villa plots, apartments and townhouses lined with trees, with themed gardens, parks with cycling lanes and a 150,000 sq. ft club house for recreation, business and entertainment. Embassy did not forget to provide for healthcare and education close by either. The other offerings here are a man-made lake, acres of promenade, a road network, green spaces, solar street lights, bus bays and acres of neighbourhood retail.

The group launched its flagship luxury branded residences by Four Seasons, called Embassy One, in 2017. This is going to be India's first Four Seasons hotel with private residences, exclusive retail outfits in the Central Plaza, and office spaces at the Pinnacle. All this is in a 7-acre space at Mekhri Circle in the heart of Bengaluru.

Embassy Splendid Techzone, a landmark property on a 30-acre land parcel on the Thoraipakkam-Pallavaram Road in Chennai is also by the group. This is along the lines of the

Embassy Manayata in Bengaluru. The total potential here is 4.5 million sq. ft; 1.11 million sq. ft of it to be completed in 2018. The group has also extended its footprint in Hyderabad, joining hands with the Phoenix Group to build parks in the most happening micro-market of Gachibowli, a major IT hub in the city.

Attaining a strong clientele of more than a 100 corporations has so far provided the group so much credibility that it plans to leverage it while launching a 300-acre integrated township in north Bengaluru and a 200-acre Embassy Knowledge Park located near the new airport. Jitu envisions it as a kind of a digitized space that people will visit even 100 years later and enjoy.

Jitu attributes his success to having great instinct and the right eye for identifying co-workers with great business sense. He's a man tight with his money, who agrees that old Sindhi habits die hard even though he makes million-dollar deals all the time. In comparison with his scale of earning, his spending is limited and he is very careful about it. Even in his busy business life he keeps an eye on his sons' expenses, knowing fully well when their spending patterns change.

A New Kid on the Block

Growing up through the family separation, Karan saw his father struggle in the business. But he has also seen the immense turnover his father's business has notched up over the years. Seeing his father work late hours and hearing the constant business chatter on the phone was like background music to Karan during his childhood. Karan studied at Mallya Aditi International School (Bengaluru) and then did business administration at University of Kent in England. He has always had an itch to make his own money.

Sanchez, the restaurant he started with a partner, came out of his hatred for asking for pocket money. Jitu had been smart, doing what his father did before him, putting his sons to work early and encouraging them to earn through small jobs. So when the idea of a restaurant came to Karan in the last year of college, nobody was surprised. Karan partnered with Siddharth Mankani. He took a loan of around Rs 3 crore from his father at 14 per cent interest to start his venture. In less than two years he returned the money. Sanchez did well due to the partners' constant surveillance, their good networking and its location.

Karan understands that his father has made enough money for the next two generations and maybe more. An 'absolute beast', is what he laughingly calls his father. He admires him unabashedly and feels lucky to be his son. It is obvious that father and son share an amazing relationship.

In September 2014, Karan started working with his father by shadowing him. He confesses, 'I did not learn anything much in business school about Indian business. Instead I learnt way more from being a fly on the wall in my father's presence, being in the actual situation, watching him deal with people, seeing him crunch numbers, watching decisions being taken at that level, all of which gave me a better understanding of the work.' Managing people, taking into consideration major professional decisions, and then being able to make calculated risks using one's instincts is the only way to go. 'Not letting failure get in one's way, crossing the hurdles one comes across and never looking back are the strengths of a true entrepreneur,' says Karan.

Jitu's inherent strength, according to his son, is that he is always positive and, like a true entrepreneur, never talks about defeat.

WeWork

Shared workspaces around the world are making news. New Indian start-ups too are realizing the need for such spaces. WeWork is an American co-working giant, with the largest network of over 120,000 members in more than 149 physical locations in fifteen countries around the world. It had been looking at the Indian market for a while when Karan brought them to his father's notice.

Karan then went on to initiate and lead the year-long negotiations with the group. WeWork met many Indian developers but decided on Embassy Group, as they felt the promoters were culturally aligned with them. Karan chose the WeWork brand and technology, as it would put Embassy on the map almost immediately. WeWork India has the DNA of both the Embassy Group, which brings in the real estate and local knowledge, and of WeWork, which contributes the brand name, and the communication and learning it has gathered through years of operations.

WeWork Galaxy (housing 2,000 desks) in Bengaluru will be the first co-working space to be started by the partnership. This city was chosen because it is demographically diverse and is referred to as the Silicon Valley of India. This will be followed by WeWork BKC (Mumbai) and then a facility in Delhi.

The smart part is that for WeWork it means a low-cost entry into India, as it is not putting in any money of its own.

Embassy will invest in the real estate, and WeWork will provide the design, technology and training for a management fee and a slice of the profits. WeWork India is a global company with a local playbook.

Jitu is happy that Karan chose something of his interest and sees the potential of a giant like WeWork in the country. When asked why Sindhis do not have big corporate business families like the Ambanis, he replies that except for the Hindujas, Sindhis haven't really ventured out on account of a few reasons. Their old school of thought creates the usual fears, such as the fear of letting go of shares of their companies, which results in the community only amassing individual wealth. For instance, if a Sindhi opened offices around the world he would plant every relative in those places to keep the money within the main family. But experience has taught Jitu otherwise, as he is now more inclined to hire professionals to run his companies, knowing very well that no developer has ever done that. Instead of having them follow the old ways, he would rather train his sons to manage professionals.

*Sources: CII Institute of Logistics, Central Statistics Office, Planning Commission, Government of India and Ports Association

Acknowledgements

Many heartfelt thanks to all the people, known and unknown, who contributed to this book.

To my father and mother who raised me to be articulate, and gifted me with the freedom of thought.

To my free-spirited son, Siddharth, and daughter, Sasha. They pushed me to be the best that I could be, never failing to remind me that I was the one.

To my ever-trusting editor, Milee Ashwarya at Penguin Random House, who saw the spark and decided the topic.

To the Sindhi community, without whom this book wouldn't have existed.

To the dream that took me into the homes and lives of these five esteemed business families who extended their extreme kindness and shared their valuable time with me.

And not to forget the people who helped me in this journey. A big thank you to: Notan Tolani, an astute businessman who led the way to the Harilelas in Hong Kong, standing by me every step of the way; Manish Lakhi for helping me connect with his busy uncle—Dilip Kumar Lakhi; Nisha Rathod, PA to Harish Fabiani, who made sure that I didn't miss any detail; Dhruv Futnani, architect and horse lover, who led me to Jitu Virwani; his amazing assistants, Hemalatha Nair and Shaina Ganpathy, who kept me on my feet during the time spent at Embassy. And all of Jitu's vertical company heads who were like warriors in disguise.

Thanks to Nitin and Dev, whose eyes shone at the mention of the matriarch of their family—Ramola Motwani.

I am truly happy that it worked out this way.

ALSO IN THE SAME SERIES

FOREWORD BY NARENDRA MODI

HOW GUJARATIS DO BUSINESS

DHANDHA

ધંધા

SHOBHA BONDRE

TRANSLATED BY SHALAKA WALIMBE

A NATIONAL BESTSELLER

Dhandha, meaning business, is a term often used in common trade parlance in India. But there is no other community that fully embodies what the term stands for than the Gujaratis.

Shobha Bondre's *Dhandha* is the story of a few such Gujaratis: Jaydev Patel—the New York Life Insurance agent credited with having sold policies worth $2.5 billion so far; Bhimjibhai Patel—one of the country's biggest diamond merchants and co-founder of the ambitious 'Diamond Naga' in Surat; Dalpatbhai Patel—the motelier who went on to become the mayor of Mansfield County; Mohanbhai Patel—a former Sheriff of Mumbai and the leading manufacturer of aluminium collapsible tubes; and Hersha and Hasu Shah—owners of over a hundred hotels in the US.

Travelling across continents—from Mumbai to the US—in search of their stories and the common values that bond them, *Dhandha* showcases the powerful ambition, incredible capacity for hard work and the inherent business sense of the Gujaratis.

'THEY HAVE AN INTRINSIC UNDERSTANDING OF MONEY
AND COMMERCE. BUSINESS IS SECOND NATURE TO THEM'
KUNAL BAHL, CEO, SNAPDEAL.COM

HOW BANIYAS DO BUSINESS

ROKDA

NIKHIL INAMDAR

Baniya—a derivative of the Sanskrit word Vanij, is a term synonymous with India's trader class. Over the decades, these capitalists spread their footprint across vast sectors of the economy, from steel and mining to telecom and retail. And now even e-tail.

Nikhil Inamdar's *Rokda* features the stories of a few pioneering men from this mercantile community—**Radheshyam Agarwal** and **Radheshyam Goenka**, founders of the cosmetic major Emami; **Rohit Bansal**, co-founder of Snapdeal; **Neeraj Gupta**, founder of Meru Cabs; and **V.K. Bansal**, a humble mathematics tutor whose genius spawned a massive coaching industry in Kota—among others.

Through the triumphs and tribulations of these men in the epoch marking India's post-independence struggle with entrepreneurship—from the License Raj to the opening up of the floodgates in 1991, and the dawn of the digital era—*Rokda* seeks to uncover the indomitable spirit of the Baniya.